MW01058211

THE GREAT
MIDWEST AMERICAN
WILD
CRITTER
COOKBOOK

by

Bruce Carlson

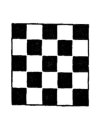 # BLACK IRON

COOKIN'

COMPANY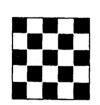

Table of Contents

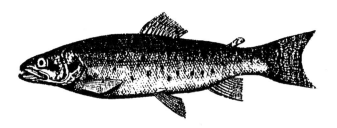

This book is dedicated to Kitty Kimble who taught me that the most important ingredient in a fish dinner is the fun you have catching the fish.

* * * * * * * * *

Quixote Press

PRINTED
IN
U.S.A.

vii

FOREWORD

THE GREAT MIDWEST AMERICAN WILD CRITTER COOKBOOK will undoubtedly prove to be the 20th Century's most definitive work on the subject.

We are all a little richer for Bruce Carlson having the ~~forsight~~ . . . ~~forsite~~ . . . ~~forsitee~~ . . . vision to see a void in our body of knowledge about cookin' and to do something about it.

Inof Splist
Literary Review Office
Journal of the Party Line
Prilspe, Hungary

FLYIN' THINGS

Index

All About Game Birds

Birds should be cleaned and frozen or cooked as soon as possible. Avoid transferring them whole in stuffy automobile trunk, as this practice does not allow for body heat to escape.

Cleaning Tips

Depending on the cooking method that is going to be used, skinning game birds is a fast and easy way to be done dressing a game bird. These birds should be used for fricasees, stews, etc.

When dry plucking a bird, pin feathers can be removed with treezers. Remaining feathers may be singed, but avoid scorching the bird's skin.

To store, wrap loosely to allow air circulation. Refrigerate at least 2-3 days before cooking, as game improves with age.

Cooked game should be stored in a covered container in refrigerator and used within 4 days.

To freeze birds, skin or pluck, draw and soak overnight in salt water. Rinse thoroughly and dry. Always wrap in moisture-vapor proof material. Try to get all air out of bags before freezing to avoid freezer burn. Store at zero degrees or lower.

Signs of Age

No old bird should be fried or broiled, so determining age can be important to the cook.

In pheasants and turkeys, an older bird can be distinguished by long, sharp spurs; the younger birds are short and pliable. The mature bird has a stiff breast bone.

Signs of Age: Mature game bird's jaws are set. An older bird can be lifted by its lower jar without signs of breaking.

Roast Pheasant

Dressed pheasant
Salt and pepper
Butter

Apples (sliced)
Bacon strips

Stuffed dressed pheasant with apples and season with salt and pepper. Cover breast with thin strips of bacon.

A fine young pheasant should be roasted at 350° about 45 minutes to 1 hour, and be generously basted with butter.

More Roast Pheasant

Pheasant (cut-up)
1 can cream of chicken soup
1 can cream of mushroom soup
1 can sherry
2 T. snipped pimiento
1 can mushrooms (drained)

Salt
Pepper
Poultry seasoning
Curry powder
1-1½ sticks margarine
Slivered almonds

Dredge pheasant in flour and brown in frying pan in 1-1½ sticks melted margarine. Season liberally with salt, pepper, poultry seasonings, and curry powder. Place in 9x12-inch pan and pour rest of mixed ingredients over it. Sprinkle top with slivered almonds, cover tightly with foil. Bake at 300° for 4 hours.

(13)

Baked Pheasant

Pheasant
1 can (small) orange juice
¼ C. brown sugar

¼ tsp. ginger
Salt and pepper

Shake pheasant pieces in flour and brown in butter. Place in baking pan. Mix orange juice with brown sugar and ginger; pour over pheasant. Season with salt and pepper. Bake until tender.

Pheasant Mulligan with Dumplings

2 young pheasants
2 C. diced carrots
1 C. diced onions
1 C. fine shredded cabbage

2 C. diced potatoes
2 T. fat
Salt and pepper

DUMPLINGS:
2 C. sifted flour
3 tsp. baking powder
½ tsp. salt

1 egg
¾ C. milk

Clean pheasant, cut into serving portions and cover with water. Add carrots, onions, and cabbage; cook slowly until nearly tender. Add potatoes, fat, salt, and pepper. Cook until meat and vegetables are tender. Add dumplings and cook for 15 minutes without lifting the cover. Serves 8.

For Dumplings: Sift flour, baking powder, and salt together. Beat egg and add milk. Stir into dry ingredients, adding more milk, if necessary, to form a drop batter. Drop by tablespoons into the hot mulligan and cover kettle tightly.

Batter Fried Pheasant

2 eggs   2 T. water

MIX:
½ C. flour   1 can mushroom soup
2 slices dried bread (crumbs)   ½ can water
Cooking oil

Beat eggs and water; refrigerate for an hour. Should be gooey. Dip pheasant pieces into egg batter and roll in flour, dip again, and roll in crumbs. Refrigerate for 2 hours. Heat ½-inch cooking oil and brown pieces on both sides. Salt pieces and place in casserole dish. Pour mushroom soup over pheasant. Cover tightly and bake at 350° for an hour.

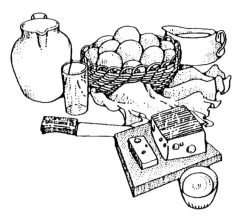

Smothered Pheasant

1 pheasant (cleaned)   ¼ tsp. pepper
½ C. flour   ½ C. cooking oil
¼ tsp. poultry seasoning   1 C. milk or light cream
½ tsp. salt

Cut pheasant into serving pieces. Combine flour and seasonings in a paper bag. Heat oil over medium heat in a large skillet. Shake pheasant in bag. Place in skillet to brown. Add milk and cover. Cook over low heat until done, about 1 hour.

Roast Pheasant

Bay leaf
Slice of lemon
Celery leaves
Bacon strips

Pheasant
White wine (if desired)
Parsley sprigs
Slice of onion

Season pheasant with salt and pepper inside and out. Cook the liver and giblets in stock until tender and chop. Reserve stock and giblets for gravy. Cover the pheasant with bacon strips and place in roaster. Add sufficient stock and white wine to cover bottom of roasting pan. Cover and cook 1 hour at 350° or until tender. Remove bacon, return to oven uncovered to permit skin to brown, basting every few minutes with juices in the pan. Remove pheasant to heated platter (and remove celery and parsley sprigs) while you prepare the gravy. Add flour to pan juices, stir until well blended, then add giblets and giblet broth. Stir and scrape sides of roaster cook slowly until thickened and pour into preheated sauce boat.

Moist Pheasant

1 pheasant (cut-up)
1 can mushroom soup
1 soup can milk

1 large sliced onion
¼ C. white wine

Roll cut-up pheasant in seasoned flour and brown; put in roaster. Mix mushroom soup, milk, and pour over pheasant. Slice onion and lay over pheasant, then pour over wine. Cover and bake at 300° for 3 hours or until tender. Always moist, this can be used for all small wild game.

Pleasant Pheasant

2 pheasants
1 (3 oz.) can mushrooms
1 T. grated cheese
2 C. uncooked rice
2 tsp. chicken seasoned
   stock base

1 C. chopped parsley
2 C. water
½ stick butter
2 T. oil
3 T. flour
Salt and pepper

Dredge pheasant parts in flour; saute' in 2 T. oil until just browned. Mix mushrooms, uncooked rice, cheese, soup base, water, parsley, salt, and pepper. Pour into greased roaster or casserole. Arrange pheasant on top. Bake, covered in 325° oven for 2 hours.

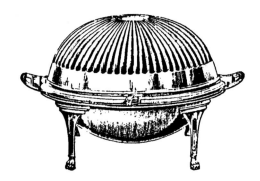

Phancy Pheasant

3 hard-cooked eggs (chopped)
4 C. cooked pheasant (chopped)
3 C. crackers (crumbled)
1 C. grated aged cheese
1 can green asparagus
½ C. melted butter

2 C. milk, plus asparagus juice
3 T. flour
Salt and pepper, to taste
½ tsp. grated lemon rind
1 can red pimientos (chopped)
1 T. butter

Melt butter, blend in flour, salt and pepper, lemon rind, stirring constantly and cook until thick. Add eggs, cheese, and pimientos. Saute' crackers in butter. In a 2-quart casserole, layer white sauce, pheasant crumbs; ending up with crumbs. Bake at 350° for 20 to 30 minutes until brown on top. Serves 6 to 8. May be baked in a 9x13-inch dish.

Pheasant in Cream

1 pheasant
3 T. margarine
Salt and pepper, to taste

1 C. cream
½ tsp. sage
1 tsp. paprika

Cut pheasant into serving pieces. Roll in flour; brown on all sides in butter or margarine. Season to taste; pour cream over; cover and simmer for 45 minutes or until tender. Serves 4.

Grandma's Pheasant Dumplings

1 pheasant
1 qt. water
Pinch of salt

1 bay leaf
½ C. chopped celery
1 T. chopped parsley

Clean and cut pheasant into serving pieces. Simmer in water and other ingredients until pheasant is tender. Cool and take meat off bones. Remove from broth to platter; drop dumplings into hot broth, cover, and cook dumplings 15 minutes. Serves 4.

Dumplings for Pheasant

2 C. flour
1½ tsp. salt

1 egg
1 C. milk

Drop by tablespoonfuls into hot pheasant broth. Cover and cook for 20 minutes. Serves 4.

Sherried Roast Pheasant

1 pheasant
1 small bay leaf
1 clove garlic
Few celery leaves
1 slice lemon

3-4 slices bacon
1 C. chicken broth
2 T. flour
3 T. dry sherry

Season inside of bird with salt. Stuff with bay leaf, garlic clove, celery leaves, lemon, and bacon slices; truss. Roast pheasant at 325° for 2 hours or until tender. Remove string and discard stuffing. Serve on bed of rice and accompany with Sherry Sauce.

For Sherry Sauce: Combine chicken broth and flour. Add to roasting pan. Stir over moderate heat, scraping loose brown drippings. When thickened, add sherry. Mix well and serve with roasted pheasant.

Mc'Pheasants

6 lbs. pheasant or turkey
   (raw, ground)
2 lbs. pork sausage
Flour

Salt, pepper and poultry
   seasoning, to taste
2 eggs (beaten)
Rolled cracker crumbs

Mix poultry meat, sausage, salt, pepper, and poultry seasoning. Form into patties. Roll patties in flour, dip in egg, and roll in cracker crumbs. Brown in skillet and finish in 325° oven for 1¾ hours. Add water as needed or add 1 can cream of mushroom soup.

Roast Pheasant with Wine

1 (1½-3 lb.) pheasant (quartered)
¼ C. flour
1½ tsp. paprika
½ tsp. salt
1/8 tsp. pepper

2 T. fat
3 oz. can mushrooms (undrained)
½ C. sauterne
¼ C. sliced onions

Combine flour, paprika, salt, and pepper. Roll phesant pieces in mixture. Brown on all sides in 2 T. fat. Add mushrooms and liquid, sauterne and onions. Cover and simmer for about 1 hour or until tender. Makes 2 to 3 servings.

Pheasant Rice Casserole

¼ C. chopped onion
1 T. butter
1 can chicken broth

1 C. cooked chopped pheasant
1 C. shredded Cheddar cheese
½ C. raw rice

Saute' onion in butter until tender. In 1½-quart casserole mix onion and butter with chicken broth, pheasant, cheese, and rice. Cover and bake at 375° for 1 hour.

Pheasant 'N Apple 'N Kraut

1½-2 lbs. pheasant
2 T. butter or margarine
1½ T. flour
1 tsp. salt
3 C. sauerkraut
½ tsp. minced onion
½ tsp. caraway seed

2 T. white wine or white
  grape juice
2 T. brown sugar
2 medium apples (tart)
  (unpeeled & wedges)
¼ C. water

Clean pheasant and pin. Soak in solution of 2 qts. water, 1 T. salt, and 1 tsp. vinegar for 2 hours to remove blood and sweeten. Cut into serving pieces. Brown in butter or margarine for 15 minutes. Remove from skillet. Blend flour into drippings. Add sauerkraut, onion, brown sugar, and seasonings. Turn into 10-cup casserole or roaster. Arrange pheasant pieces on top of kraut. Add water. Cover and bake in moderate oven at 350° for 45 minutes. Cut apples into wedges, core, and arrange around pheasant. Add wine and cover. Return to oven and bake for 25 minutes or until pheasant is tender. Garnish with fresh parsley. Serves 3 to 4.

Roast Pheasant in Dressing

1 dressed pheasant (2-3 lbs.)
3½-4 C. cubed bread
¾ C. chopped celery
½ C. chopped onion
2 T. margarine
½ C. water

⅔ C. milk
1 egg (slightly beaten)
2 tsp. sage
⅔ tsp. salt
Dash of black pepper

Remove pin feathers and singe. Soak in solution of 1 qt. water, 1 T. salt, and 1 tsp. vinegar for 2 hours. Rinse thoroughly and drain. Saute' onion and celery in margarine for 5 minutes. Add water. Tear bread into chunks. Add milk, seasonings, egg, and cooled onions and celery. Toss lightly to mix and pack into salted cavity of pheasant; truss. Lay 3 strips of bacon over breast and top of legs and place breast up in roaster rack. Cover and bake in moderate slow oven at 325° for about 2 hours. Remove cover and roast for ½ hour longer to brown pheasant. Remove pheasant from roaster and use drippings to make gravy. (Be sure to lay strips of bacon or pork over breast because pheasants are dry.) Serves 4.

Pheasants & Veggies

Dress, wash, and drain well. Cover each breast with a grape leaf or coating of lard. Braise pheasant in a good condensed stock. Blanch 1 head of cabbage, cut in wedges; braise this with some smoked sausage, a piece of salt pork, 2 carrots, 1 bay leaf, a large onion, and 2 whole cloves. (Use 6 carrots.) When cabbage is done, remove bay leaf and cloves. Keep warm until pheasant is done. Debone the 2 pheasants, arrange on platter with vegetables. Serve with stock from pheasant and vegetables that have been strained through cheesecloth. Serve all with Madeira Sauce.

For Sauce: Cook a few peppercorns in glass of Maderia wine; strain. Add 3 chopped onions, 2 carrots, ½ clove of garlic, 4 mushrooms, 2 T. butter, and a teaspoon of tomato paste. Cook until vegetables are well done. Strain through cheesecloth. Mix together, heat, and thicken with 4 beaten egg yolks.

Aunt Joy's Pheasant and Dumplings

2 pheasants	2 C. or more diced potatoes
2 C. diced carrots	2 T. fat
1 C. diced onions	Salt and pepper, to taste
1 C. finely shredded cabbage	

DUMPLINGS:

2 C. sifted flour	¼ tsp. caraway seed
3 tsp. baking powder	1 egg
½ tsp. salt	¾ C. milk
¼ tsp. dry mustard	Dash of sage

Clean pheasants, cut into serving pieces and cover with water. Add vegetables and cook slowly until almost tender. Add potatoes, fat, salt, and pepper. Cook until meat is tender. Make the dumplings. Sift together dry ingredients, beat egg and add milk to egg and caraway seed; mix well. Drop by spoonfuls into hot broth. Cover and cook for 15 to 20 minutes.

Pheasant 'N Rice

Cut-up pheasant
1 can cream of celery soup
1 can cream of mushroom soup
1 can milk (use soup can to measure)

1 pkg. Lipton's dry onion soup
1 pkg. Uncle Ben's wild &
  long grain rice

Mix all ingredients together, except pheasant. Pour mixture into 9x13-inch baking dish. Lay pheasant on top and cover with foil. Bake at 325° for 2 hours. Uncover the last half hour.

Pheasant 'N Wild Rice

1 can mushrooms & juice
1 box Uncle Ben's long
  grain & wild rice

1 can chicken broth
1 pheasant (cut-up or whole)
Mrs. Dash

In a 9x13-inch pan put rice, mushrooms, mushroom juice, and chicken broth. Mix well. Lay pheasant (it's easier cut-up) on top and sprinkle with Mrs. Dash. Bake at 3500 for 1 hour.

Pheasant, Veggies and Gravy

In baking dish put pheasant (whole). Add 1 env. Lipton Onion soup and 1 quart water. Add carrots, onion, celery (with tops) and apple. Bake at 350° for 1½ hours. Take pheasant and vegetables out. Boil liquid, add cornstarch to make gravy. (Note: Place pheasant breast side down; this helps to keep breast from drying out.)

Pheasant Breasts

Breast of 2 pheasants   *2 C. corn flake crumbs or*
2 eggs   *cracker crumbs*

Debone pheasant breast, remove tendons, tenderize with meat tenderizing hammer. Dip in beaten egg and roll in crumbs. Fry in oil until golden brown. Good served on buns.

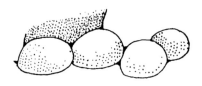

Phesant Ala Whipping Cream

1 pheasant   *1 carton whipping cream*

Cut-up pheasant like chicken. Flour and fry. Place in pressure cooker. Cover with 1 carton of whipping cream or heavy cream. Pressurize for 20 minutes.

Fried Fowl

¼ C. margarine   *1 C. apple juice*
¼ tsp. thyme   *1 tsp. salt*
¼ C. chopped onion   *1/8 tsp. paprika*
1 tsp. dried parsley   *Flour*

Quarter bird and roll in flour. Melt the margarine in a heavy frypan. When it is hot brown the fowl. Sprinkle on the thyme. Cover and cook over low heat for 10 minutes. Mix the chopped onion, dried parsley, and cup of juice which may be from cooked dried apples. Cover and keep simmering for 1 hour. About 10 minutes before the cooking is finished, sprinkle on salt and paprika. A good accompaniment is rice.

Plesant Pheasant Casserole

2 beaten eggs
2 C. broth (from cooking pheasant)
1 can mushroom soup
½ C. chopped onion
¼ tsp. salt

¾ C. chopped celery
¾ C. grated American cheese
2½ C. crushed Ritz crackers
Boned pheasant
¼ tsp. pepper

Cook 1 pheasant in salt water until tender. Save broth. Mix all ingredients, turn into buttered baking dish and bake at 350° for 1 hour.

Pheasant 'N Mushroom

1 dressed pheasant
1 can Campbell's Golden
  Mushroom soup

¼ C. water

Place pheasant, soup, and water in crock pot. Cook on High for 4 hours or Low for 6 hours. Carefully remove all bones from meat and sauce. Great when served with bread and mashed potatoes. Serves family of 4.

Square Pheasant

Filet of pheasant breasts
  from 2 pheasants
1 C. flour
1 tsp. baking powder

½ tsp. salt
1 egg
1 C. milk
¼ C. salad oil

Cut pheasant breasts into 1-inch square pieces. Mix remaining ingredients to form batter. Beat until smooth. Dip pieces into batter and deep fat fry until golden brown. Salt and serve. Serves family of 4.

More Breasts of Pheasant

Breasts of 2 pheasants (dressed)   *1 tsp. grated onion*
4 slices ham   *½ tsp. rosemary*
1 tsp. salt   *½ lb. mushrooms (sliced thin)*
½ tsp. butter   *2 T. flour*

Cut breasts from bone, leaving skin on. Dust with salt and cayenne. Brown well on both sides in deep butter with onion and rosemary for 8 to 10 minutes. Keep warm in a covered pan in a very slow oven, 250°, while you saute' ham in same butter. Put one breast on each slice of ham. Saute' mushrooms in the same skillet for 3 minutes. Push mushrooms to one side of the pan; pour off all but about 2 T. butter. Add flour, blend, and add chicken broth. When smooth and thick, pour over birds. Adjust seasoning. Serves 4.

Ploured Pheasant

Clean bird; cut up. Roll in seasoned flour. In oven, brown pieces slowly on both sides in ½ C. hot fat, turning once. Top with 2 C. sliced onion. Pour over 1 C. water, milk or light cream. Cover tightly. Cook on top of range over low heat or bake at 325° until tender, about 1 hour. Make gravy from drippings. Serves 3 or 5.

Creamed Pheasant

1 pheasant, dressed	¼ C. oil or margarine
⅓ C. flour	1 C. cream
1 C. water	1 tsp. minced onion
1 tsp. salt	Pinch of thyme
¼ tsp. black pepper	

Clean and remove pin feathers, singe pheasant. Soak in solution of 2 qts. water, 1 T. salt, and 1 tsp. vinegar. Rinse thoroughly and drain; cut into serving pieces. Dredge in flour, salt, and pepper. Brown slowly on all sides in oil or margarine, about 10 to 15 minutes. Blend in any remaining flour and thyme in oil in pan. Add water and simmer for 1 hour, covered. Add onion and cream and simmer until tender. Serve with boiled potatoes with jackets on. Serves 4 to 5. Garnish with paprika and parsley.

Note: For sour pheasant, substitute sour cream for sweet cream, dill weed for thyme, and add ¼ to ½ tsp. sugar.

Braised Pheasant in Sour Cream

1 dressed pheasant	¼ tsp. sugar
3 T. flour	½ tsp. paprika
1½ tsp. salt	1 C. sour cream
3 T. butter	Onion, if desired
1½ C. water	

Clean pheasant. Be sure to remove pin feathers. Rinse well and drain. Cut into serving pieces. Dredge in flour, salt, and pepper. Brown slowly on all sides in butter. Blend only remaining flour into butter in the pan. Add ¼-½ C. water and blend until smooth. Lower heat, cover, and simmer for 1¾ hours or until tender. Adding remaining water as needed. Add remaining ingredients and blend well. Simmer gently for 15 minutes. Simmer onions for the full cooking time.

Kraut Pheasant with Apple

1 dressed pheasant	2 medium tart apples (peeled)
1½ tsp. salt	¼ C. water
2 T. shortening	4 tsp. white wine
3½ C. sauerkraut	¼-½ tsp. caraway seed
2 T. brown sugar	

Clean pheasant and rinse well; drain. Cut into pieces. Sprinkle with salt. Brown slowly on all sides in butter. Remove pheasant from skillet and blend flour into drippings in pan. Add sauerkraut and brown sugar; mix to blend thoroughly. Turn into 10-cup casserole. Arrange the brown pheasant on top of kraut. Cut the apples into chunks. Arrange on top of pheasant. Add water, cover, and bake at 350° for 1 hour. Sprinkle wine and caraway seed over pheasant. Cover and bake for 30 more minutes.

Pheasant in a Blanket

1 dressed pheasant

VEGETABLE STUFFING:

¾ C. grated carrots	1 C. chopped celery
½ chopped onion	1½ T. chopped parsley
¼ C. chopped chives	Salt and pepper

DOUGH TO WRAP PHEASANT IN:

1½ C. flour	2 T. shortening
1 tsp. salt	½ C. water

Clean pheasant getting rid of pin feathers and hair. Rinse and soak in salt water for several hours; drain. Mix vegetables and fill pheasant. Mix dough to wrap pheasant as you would pie crust. Roll out and wrap pheasant completely sealing edges tight; so pheasant is all encased. Place pheasant, breast side up, in shallow roaster; roast uncovered in an oven of 325° for 2½ hours. Prepare gravy from drippings. Break away crust in pieces and serve with pheasant and gravy. Serves 4.

Aunt Hattie's Pheasant

1 pheasant
½ C. butter
1 T. dried chives
1 tsp. rosemary
1 T. parsley flakes
½ C. orange juice (undiluted)

½ C. white wine
1 C. water
1 C. rice (regular, not minute)
Salt and pepper
1 orange (sliced in rounds)

Quarter pheasant, place in large skillet and brown in butter. Add chives, salt, pepper, and remaining spices. Add juice, wine, and water. Cover and cook over low heat for ½ hour. Add rice, cover, and cook for ½ hour. About 5 minutes before serving, add orange slices and cover to warm. Serves 2.

Mom's Baked Pheasant

2 pheasants (cut-up)
Flour
Oil

Salt and pepper
Water

Flour all pieces. Brown in oil in frying pan. Place browned pieces in roaster. Salt and pepper. Add enough water to cover the bottom of pan. Cover and bake at 350° for 1 hour or until done.

Our Neighbor's Pheasant Recipe

1 pheasant (browned)
2 potatoes (cubed, boiled to
  almost tender stage)

1 can mixed vegetables
1 can cream of mushroom soup
Water

Brown pheasant, cut-up if desired, place in large enough roaster to allow for vegetables. Bake or cook until pheasant is tender. Add cubed potatoes, water if necessary, mixed vegetables, and soup. Continue cooking until potatoes are tender and warmed thoroughly.

Tipsy Pheasant

1 pheasant
Croutons
1 orange

Salt and pepper
1 jar orange marmalade
1 bottle white cooking wine

Wash bird and pat dry. Salt and pepper. Stuff with croutons and orange slices. Pour about 2 C. white wine over bird and place in 350° oven in covered roasting pan. Cook for approximately 2 hours basting bird with orange marmalade while cooking.

Still More Pheasant

Pheasant (cut into serving pieces)
Seasoned flour
  (salt, pepper & paprika)

½ C. fat for frying
2 C. onions (sliced)
1 C. milk or light cream

Roll pieces of pheasant in seasoned flour. In Dutch oven, brown pieces slowly on both sides in the hot fat, turning once. Top with 2 C. sliced onions. Pour the milk or light cream over the top and cover tightly. Simmer over low heat or bake at 325° until tender (about 1 hour). Make gravy from drippings. Quail or Grouse can be done this way, only cooking a shorter time.

Bird Stew

2 whole game birds
¼ C. butter or margarine
4 cubes chicken bouillon
4 C. water
1 small pkg. frozen broccoli or
  equivalent amount of fresh
  broccoli (chopped)
½ C. milk

4 medium carrots
  (peeled & sliced)
1 small onion
2 medium potatoes
  (unpeeled, scrubbed & cubed)
1 handful egg noodles
1 can mushroom soup

Place water, bouillon, butter, and meat in large pot. Simmer until meat is tender (about 45 minutes), adding water if necessary. Remove the meat from the broth; add the vegetables and egg noodles and simmer until all are tender. While vegetables are cooking, remove meat from the bones; tear it into small pieces and add to broth. Add soup and milk to broth and heat through. Make sure the stew does not come to a boil. Serves 4.

Burnt Bluebills

6 bluebills
10 ozs. Italian dressing

1 onion
8 hamburger buns

Fillet out breasts of ducks by peeling back skin and taking meat only. Soak fillets in dressing overnight after beating each with tenderizer (pope hammer). Remove from marinade, salt, and pepper; barbecue over charcoal 4 minutes on a side. Serve on buttered buns with slice of onion. Be sure to not overcook. Makes a great lunch on a duck hunt. Can easily be carried to the blind. Serves 4.

Yummy Duck Jerky

Duck breasts   *Salt*
Liquid smoke

Cut dressed duck breasts as thin as possible or 1/8-inch thick. Dip in liquid smoke and salt. Hang strips on the top grate of the oven with toothpicks poked in the ends of strips. Line the bottom grate with aluminum foil to catch drips. Bake at 300° for 6 hours or until done, with oven door cracked open so the steam escapes.

Pigeon Pie

1 recipe pastry   *6 carrots (diced)*
4 pigeons (parboiled)   *½ C. tomato paste*
3 T. flour   *2 C. stock pigeons, boiled in:*
2 stalks celery (diced)   *¼ tsp. thyme*
2 onions (sliced)   *½ clove garlic (mashed)*
2 T. fat   *¾ C. milk*

Line a deep casserole with pastry. Fry parboiled pigeons in fat until lightly brown. Place fried pigeons in casserole. Fry vegetables in pan with drippings from pigeons. When tender, place in casserole with pigeons. Thicken drippings after adding stock and milk; add seasonings and pour over pigeons. Cover with buttered bread crumbs. Bake at 450° for 10 minutes, reduce heat, and bake for another hour. Serves 4.

Rice 'N Roast Pigeon Breasts

6 slices bacon
¾ C. celery (diced)
1 onion (chopped)
2 C. uncooked rice
4 C. chicken stock

4 eggs
Salt and pepper
4 pigeon breasts
Mustard pickle juice

Dice bacon and fry crisp. Remove bacon and add onion and celery to bacon drippings; brown lightly. Boil rice in chicken stock; add onions and celery. Beat eggs and add. Season to taste. In greased casserole, arrange pigeons. Pile mounds of rice mixture on breasts and around. Bake at 325° for 45 to 60 minutes. Baste every 15 minutes with mustard pickle juice.

Pigeon Pots

6 pigeons or doves
4 C. sage stuffing
3 slices bacon
1 carrot (diced)
1 onion (diced)
1 tsp. parsley (chopped)

4 C. hot water with 2 chicken
  bouillon cubes added
¼ C. oleo
¼ C. flour
6 slices buttered toast

Place birds in roaster, stuff with dressing and lay birds on bacon. Add carrots, onions, and parsley. Add water mixed with bouillon, 2 cups. Cover and bake for 2 to 3 hours. Melt fat and blend in flour and add remaining 2 C. stock. Cook this separately in saucepan. Serve each bird on toast with vegetables and pour gravy over.

"Real Good" Deviled Pigeons

Cut slashes in breast of pigeons   *1/8 tsp. cayenne pepper*
1 T. mustard (prepared)

CREAM TOGETHER THE FOLLOWING:
½ C. butter   *¼ tsp. salt*
2 tsp. mustard   *Dash of cayenne*
2 tsp. Worcestershire sauce

Cut the breasts of pigeons - rub in mustard and cayenne. Broil until brown-ed and tender. Mix ingredients of sauce in pan; heat until just boils, serve hot over broiled breasts.

Pigeons 'N Sour Cream

4 pigeon breasts or whole pigeons   *½ tsp. paprika*
¼ C. flour   *Pinch of basil*
2 T. butter   *White pepper*
½ C. diced onion   *1 can mushroom pieces*
½ C. tomato juice or paste   *1 C. dairy sour cream*
½ tsp. salt   *Dash of lemon juice*
1 tsp. parsley (chopped)

Pat pigeons dry; coat with flour. In hot butter, brown pigeons 10 to 15 minutes. Add onion and cook until tender. Combine tomato juice, lemon juice, parsley, basil, salt, pepper, and drained mushrooms. Bring to a boil; reduce heat and cook until tender. Remove pigeons and place on platter and keep hot; add sour cream to tomato mixture. Reheat very gently. Pour over pigeons.

Spiced Pigeons with Hot Sauce

6 pigeons
Make 4 C. sage dressing
6 link sausages
⅔ C. salad olives
2 cloves garlic (minced)
1 can mushroom pieces

3 T. salad oil
½ tsp. basil
1 (8 oz.) can tomato sauce
½ tsp. chopped parsley
1 tsp. chopped onion
¼ tsp. hot sauce (if desired)

Stuff pigeons with dressing. Brown sausages, remove, and add remaining ingredients and simmer for 10 minutes. Place pigeons in roaster and arrange sausages around. Pour over the tomato sauce, cover, and roast at 400° for 30 minutes; basting every 20 minutes. Reduce heat to 375° and roast for 40 minutes more basting every 10 minutes. Serve with cooked rice.

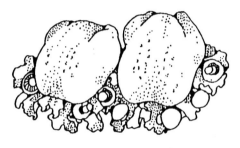

Tipsy Quail

2 small onions
½ C. fat
1 tsp. peppercorns
2 whole cloves
2 cloves garlic (cut fine)
6 quail
½ bay leaf

2 C. white wine
1/8 tsp. pepper
½ tsp. salt
1 tsp. minced chives
Few grains cayenne
2 C. cream of evaporated milk

Melt fat; add cloves, peppercorns, garlic, bay leaf, and onions. Cook for several minutes. Add quail and brown. Add salt and pepper, cayenne, wine, and chives. Simmer for about 40 minutes. Remove quail; strain sauce and add cream and heat to boiling point. Pour over quail. Serves 2.

Broiled Partridge

Split partridge in two and remove breast bone. Flatten, season with pepper and salt. Dip in melted butter and roll in bread crumbs. Boil for 18 to 20 minutes. Serve with lemon slices.

Old Fashioned Partridge

Use 2 portions of breast. Roll each piece in 2 slices of bacon; season with pepper and salt. Broil for 10 minutes. Place on slices of toast; add 3 cooked mushrooms to each serving. Good potatoes. Serve hot.

Breast of Partridge

Use breast of 3 partridges. Remove skin, season breasts with sage and rosemary leaves. Roll in 2 strips. Grill for 20 minutes on charcoal broiler.

Quail Dressing

1 quail per serving
⅓ C. chopped onion
¼ C. butter
⅓ C. chopped celery
½ tsp. poultry seasoning

¼ lb. day-old white bread
2 T. chopped parsley
½ tsp. salt
Strips of bacon

Heat butter; add celery and onion. Saute' until onion is soft, about 5 minutes. Add bread, seasonings, and parsley to celery and onion. Drizzle milk over mixture and mix lightly with fork. Place dressing in greased casserole; place quail on top of dressing. Put casserole in pan of hot water and bake, covered at 350° for 45 to 50 minutes. Uncover and bake 10 more minutes or until tender to brown quail.

Lemon Partridge

3 partridges
½ C. wine

¼ C. lemon juice

Place clean, larded bird in greased casserole; add lemon juice and bake at 350° for 15 minutes. Add wine, cover, and cook until tender or about 25 minutes. Serve with lemon sauce. Serves 6.

Baked Tipsy Quail

6 quail
½ C. fat
2 small onions
2 whole cloves
2 cloves garlic

½ bay leaf
2 C. wine
½ tsp. salt
¼ tsp. pepper
2 C. cream or evaporated milk

Brown birds in fat, onions, cloves, garlic, and bay leaf. Cook several minutes. Add wine, salt, and pepper; simmer until tender, about 30 minutes. Remove quail; strain sauce. Add cream and heat to boiling; pour over quail.

Roast Quail

4 dressed quail
6 T. butter
Salt
Pepper
3 T. cognac

1 C. chicken stock
1-2 tsp. lemon juice
30 white grapes (halved & seeded)
2 apples (sliced)
¼ C. vermouth

Rub quail generously with butter, salt, and pepper. Put a lump of butter, ½ of apple (sliced) or 4 white grapes in cavities. Sprinkle with cognac. Roast at 400° for 15 minutes, basting every 5 minutes. While quail are roasting, gently heat seeded and halved grapes in vermouth and chicken stock. Remove grapes and add these to quail; roast another 15 minutes. Remove quail to heated serving platter. Add the vermouth and chicken stock to pan juices with lemon juice. Stir well. Pour sauce over quail. Garnish and serve.

Quail

Take a roasting pan, butter it liberally with melted butter. Season the quail with salt and pepper and any other seasonings desired; place in the pan and cover them with melted butter. Lay strips of bacon on each bird. Place in hot oven (475°) and bake for another 15 minutes. Reduce heat moderate heat (350°) and bake until done. During the baking, be sure to baste often with the juices and butter. Can be served with gravy made from the juices or in any other way desired.

Wild Rice and Dove or Quail
(In Season)

8-10 dressed birds
2 C. wild rice
1 tsp. salt
2 C. water
1 T. crushed sage

1 large onion (chopped)
1 can mushroom soup
Pepper
Chicken broth
Cream of chicken soup (optional)

Brown birds in small amount of shortening. Cook rice in water until tender. Mix all but birds together. Add enough broth to moisten. Pour in baking dish. Arrange birds on top of rice. Bake at 325°, covered for 1 hour, then uncover and bake for 15 minutes to brown.

Quail Kabobs

15 quail breasts (deboned)
4 large green peppers
6 small onions

1 lb. bacon
1 stick butter or margarine (melted)
¼ C. lemon juice

Cut ingredients in equal size pieces. Place on kabob skewers in this order: onion, quail, pepper, and bacon. Repeat until skewer is full. Place on BBQ grill on low flame, brush on butter and lemon juice which has been mixed. Turn and brush often. Keep moist.

Quail Pie

Make a rich biscuit dough, using milk or cream for mixing. Roll thin; spread with butter, fold, and roll again. Line a baking pan with the dough. Split dressed quail down the back, lay them in the pan and sprinkle with salt and pepper; spread each bird with butter. Add boiling water, about ⅔ C. to each bird. Cover with crust and make some small slits to let out steam, and bake in medium oven until done.

Quail and Wild Rice

5-6 quail
6 oz. pkg. Uncle Ben's long
  grain & wild rice
⅓ C. onion (chopped)
¼ C. margarine

⅓ C. flour
1 tsp. salt
Dash of pepper
1 C. Half 'N Half or whole milk
1 C. quail broth

Stew quail until tender, about 1 hour. Remove meat from bones. Cook rice according to package directions, using foil packet of seasonings. Saute' onion and green pepper in margarine. Add flour, salt, and pepper; stir to blend. Gradually stir in cream and broth. Cook until thickened. Mix all and put in a greased 2-quart casserole. Bake at 350° for about 1 hour.

Fried Quail

Cut-up quail as desired. (It is usually best to have three pieces — breast and two legs. (Season with salt and pepper; roll pieces in flour. Place in hot deep fat and brown quickly on both sides. Turn down heat and cover pan; let cook slowly until tender. Make gravy right in the same skillet using residue left from frying.

Oven Quail

6 dressed quail
Flour
Butter or shortening

Salt
Pepper

Roll moistened quail in flour. Brown on top of stove in small amount of shortening or butter. Put in oven with ¼ C. butter. Baste quail every 20 minutes or so. Bake at 325°-350° for 1 hour. Salt and pepper, to taste. Serves family of 4.

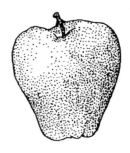

Orangy Roast Duck

1 duck
1 apple
1 onion

1 carrot
1 stalk celery

To dress and clean duck. Soak in solution of 1 qt. water, 1 T. baking soda for 2 to 3 hours. Rinse duck thoroughly and drain. Sprinkle duck with salt and pepper. Place onion, celery, apple, and carrot in duck. Over breast of duck place 2 or 3 strips of bacon. Truss duck. Arrange duck on roasting rack. Bake, uncovered at 350°, basting occasionally. Roast for 15 to 20 minutes per pound. Discard onion, celery, and carrot. Serve duck with Hot Orange Sauce. Garnish with slices of oranges and parsley.

Sweet and Sour Goose

2 geese (quartered)
½ C. pineapple juice
¼ C. wine vinegar
1 C. apple juice
Flour

2 T. oil
¼ C. brown sugar
¼ C. lemon juice
Can of pineapple chunks
 (drained)

Mix all ingredients and marinade goose for several hours. Remove goose, pat dry and roll in flour. Brown in oil and place in roaster. Pour pineapple chunks over goose. Add marinade mixture and roast at 325° for 2 hours. Serve with sauce. May thicken sauce with cornstarch.

"I know this isn't a very good picture of a goose, but it's the best I can do this morning."

Orange Sauce

1½ C. beef stock
2 oranges
1 lemon
¼ C. butter
½ C. water

¼ C. flour
½ tsp. salt
Dash cayenne pepper
2 T. sherry wine

Slice the peel of 1 orange as fine as possible. Cook in water for 5 minutes; put in saucepan with 1 C. beef stock. Brown the butter and add flour and seasonings. Stir until browned. Add rest of beef stock. Gradually add the juice of lemon and oranges, then orange rind mixture. Boil a few minutes. Just before serving add sherry. You may add a spoonful of currant jelly. Serve hot over roasted duck.

Sausage-Stuffed Wild Duck

STUFFING:

½ lb. unseasoned pork sausage
¼ C. grated onion
½ C. fine-cut celery
1 T. minced parsley
2 T. grated green pepper
1½ C. cold water

½ tsp. pepper
1 tsp. salt
4 C. dry bread cubes
½ tsp. sage or poultry seasoning
¼ C. melted butter

Mix well the first 8 ingredients and cook for 30 to 45 minutes. Remove from heat and cool until grease sets. Remove as much of the grease as possible. Add bread cubes, sage or poultry seasoning, and melted butter. Toss to mix well, adding more moisture if necessary, milk or water.

To Prepare Duck: Rub inside of duck lightly with salt. Put stuffing lightly into cavity and skewer or lace opening. Brush outside with soft shortening and dust with flour. Place in covered roasting pan, breast side up and roast in 325° oven for 3½ to 4 hours or until breast meat starts to fall off bone. Baste at 45 minutes intervals, and season with salt and pepper. Serves 2.

Roast Duck and Apple Stuffing

2 large mallard ducks
½ C. chopped celery
½ C. chopped onion
2 medium apples (chopped)
¼ C. brown sugar
¼ C. chopped walnuts
2-4 slices bread (cubed)

¼ C. raisins
Dash of pepper
½ tsp. salt
1/8 tsp. marjoram
Dash of sage
1 bouillon cube
1 C. warm water

Soak ducks overnight in salt water brine. Drain and place in roaster. Dissolve bouillon in water. Add ½ C. bouillon to remaining ingredients. Place stuffing around ducks. Pour remaining bouillon over ducks. Bake for 1½ hours or until done at 325°.

Wild Duck

5 Jonathan apples
Bacon strips
Ducks (2 Mallards)

1 C. raisins
Salt and pepper
Spices

Season ducks with salt and pepper inside and out. Don't peel apple, quarter them, and place some apples and some raisins in each duck. Place ducks in roasting pan and put the rest of the apples and raisins around them. Add the spices which you favor. Place bacon strips on each duck. Pour about 1½ C. of water into the pan. Bake at 350° until tender. Add more water, if needed.

Roast Duck with Apple Stuffing

2 large Mallard ducks
½ C. chopped celery
½ C. chopped onion
2 medium apples (cut-up)
¼ C. brown sugar
¼ C. chopped walnuts
2 to 4 slices bread (cubed)

¼ C. raisins
Dash of pepper
½ tsp. salt
1/8 tsp. marjoram
Dash of sage
1 bouillon cube
1 C. warm water

Soak ducks overnight in salt and water brine. Drain and place in roasting pan. Mix celery, onion, apples, brown sugar, walnuts, bread cubes, raisins, and seasonings. Dissolve bouillon cube in 1 C. warm water; add ½ C. bouillon to dressing mixture to moisten. Place dressing around ducks. Pour remaining bouillon over ducks. Bake at 325° for 1 hour and 30 minutes or until done. Serves 4.

BBQ Wild Duck

2 ducks, dressed

MARINADE:

½ C. lemon juice

1½ C. oil

½ tsp. thyme

½ tsp. celery seed

1 clove garlic (minced)

Place ducks in marinade for 10 to 12 hours. Remove from marinade and place in roasting pan. Bake at 350° for 20 minutes, uncovered. Pour ½ of barbecue sauce over and around ducks. Cover and bake until ducks are tender, 20 minutes per pound of duck. Serve with hot barbecue sauce over ducks. Garnish with onion slices and lemon wedges.

BARBECUE SAUCE:

½ C. oil

1½ C. tomato juice

4 T. vinegar

1 clove garlic (minced)

1 T. minced onion

Few drops Tabasco sauce

½ tsp. salt

1 tsp. Worcestershire sauce

1 T. prepared mustard

Dash of red pepper

½ tsp. chili powder

Pinch of paprika

½ tsp. sugar

Mix ingredients together. Heat to boiling. Simmer for 2 minutes. Makes 2 cups.

Roast Grouse

Clean bird and wipe with damp cloth. Cover with salt pork and or bacon. Roast in 350° oven for about 1 hour. Baste from time to time. Thicken juices for gravy.

Broiled Grouse

Parboil grouse for 30 minutes. Baste with melted margarine and place under broiler until tender.

Dove Pie

6 doves
Salt and pepper
1 qt. water
½ onion (chopped)
¼ C. minced parsley
¼ lb. salt pork (diced)

2 whole cloves
2 T. fat
2 T. flour
½ recipe pastry
2 C. diced cooked potatoes

Clean birds and split in halves. Cover with water and heat to boiling. Add salt pork, cloves, onion, parsley, salt, and pepper. Simmer, keeping birds covered with water until tender. Thicken liquid with flour and heat gravy to boiling. Add fat; take from heat and cool. Put birds in casserole; add potatoes and gravy. Cover with crust, with holes poked in it. Bake at 425° for 15 to 20 minutes. Serves 10.

Roast Wild Turkey

Roast turkey with favorite stuffing. For more flavor and juiciness, roast breast down; if roasted breast up, cover breast with strips of bacon or fat salt pork or melted butter. Roast in moderate oven, 20 to 25 minutes per pound.

Fried Wild Turkey

3 lb. dressed turkey   *2 tsp. salt*
2 tsp. paprika   *¼ tsp. pepper*
½ C. flour

Shake turkey in bag until each piece is coated. Melt ½-inch of fat in heavy skillet; add turkey and brown well. Reduce heat, cover, and continue cooking about 1 hour. Remove cover and continue cooking for 5 minutes to crisper doneness. Caraway seeds may be added.

Wild Turkey Strips

1 turkey   *Water*
½ C. salt   *4 eggs*
½ C. brown sugar   *½ C. milk*
2 bay leaves   *Cracker crumbs*
Oil

Soak whole turkey for 2 days in a cool place in ½ C. salt, ½ C. brown sugar, 2 bay leaves, and water to cover bird; drain. Slice strips of meat off bird. Mix eggs and milk. Roll meat in egg and milk mixture and then in cracker crumbs. Fry in oil. Can be fixed, put in layers in freezer dish with freezer paper between layers and freeze. When frozen, put in plastic bags and return to freezer. Reheat for a quick meal. Cook bones for soup.

Curried Goose

Breast from 1 goose
½ C. flour
¼ tsp. pepper
¼ tsp. paprika
1 onion (diced)

½ tsp. salt
2 T. curry
1 C. chicken broth
6 T. butter

Cut breast fillets in bite-size pieces. Coat with flour, pepper, and paprika. Saute' lightly in butter; remove grease. Saute' onions in butter and add flour, salt, curry, and broth. Return goose: reduce heat and simmer, covered for 45 minutes. Remove lid and simmer for 5 more minutes. Serve over rice. Serves 4.

Liver Pate' From Wild Flyin' Things

½ lb. livers (adjust other
   ingredients to match quantity
   of livers)
1 onion (diced)
Clove of garlic
2 hard-boiled eggs (finely diced)
1 T. grated onion

2 T. mayonnaise
1 tsp. vinegar
Dash of Worcestershire sauce
Salt and pepper, to taste
½ tsp. dry mustard
Pinch of sugar

Save all livers (duck, quail, pheasant, etc.). Simmer in salted water for ½ hour. Add onion and clove of garlic. Cook slowly for 1 hour. Remove liver and discard garlic clove. Mash liver and mix with eggs, grated onion, mayonnaise, vinegar, Worcestershire sauce, salt, pepper, dry mustard, and sugar. Serve on crackers.

(47)

Wild Goose

Clean and pick goose well — do not skin. Lay the giblets to one side to use in the stuffing. Prepare stuffing as follows:

2½ qt. stale bread	*2 Jonathan apples (diced)*
(broken up)	*Salt and pepper*
Goose giblets	*Sage*
1 large onion (chopped fine)	*Garlic*

Boil giblets till tender, remove skin, and chop fine. Combine with bread, onions, and apple. Mix well and add salt and pepper, sage, garlic, and other seasonings to taste. Moisten and stuff goose. Place goose in roasting pan and spread with about 2 T. of butter and then sprinkle with a little flour. Roast in 350° oven until done, which will take about 15 to 20 minutes per pound. Baste often.

Wild Turkey Hash

¼ C. chopped onion	*1½ C. rich turkey broth*
¼ C. chopped green pepper	*Salt and pepper, to taste*
2 T. butter	*1½ C. leftover dressing*
2 C. chopped turkey	*3 C. cubed cooked potatoes*

Saute' onion and green pepper in butter for 10 minutes until yellow and transparent. Add remaining ingredients and mix lightly. Heat thoroughly and serve immediately.

Grilled Dove

Dove breast (split)
Jalapeno peppers (sliced)
1 stick butter or oleo (melted)

¼ C. lemon juice
Bacon

Fill dove breast with peppers. Wrap with 1 slice of bacon. Secure with toothpick through middle to hold together. Place on BBQ grill on low flame. Turn and baste often with butter and lemon juice mixed.

Roasted Wild Goose with Sauerkraut

1 wild goose (dressed)
Sauerkraut

Butter
Salt and pepper

Stuff goose with sauerkraut and rub a little butter on the outside; salt and pepper. Bake at 350° until tender. Serve the sauerkraut with the goose. The goose will not taste of the kraut, it only makes it moist and improves the flavor.

(49)

Thanksgiving Roast Wild Turkey
With All the Extras

THE STOCK:
Turkey giblets and neck

THE STUFFING:
½ lb. sausage (crumbled)	*1 bay leaf*
1 large onion (chopped)	*2 C. chestnuts*
2 ribs celery & leaves (diced)	*(peeled & cooked)*
½ green pepper (chopped)	*½ tsp. thyme*
4 T. butter	*4 tsp. sage*
3 C. dried bread cubes	*¾ tsp. salt*
Freshly ground pepper	

THE TURKEY:
1 big Tom Turkey	*Softened butter*
½ C. lemon	*½ C. white wine*
Salt and pepper	

For The Stock: Make a stock first by putting giblets and neck to boil with bay leaf, then simmer for 20 minutes.

For The Stuffing: Meanwhile saute' the crumbled sausage. Add the three vegetables and saute' in butter until onions and peppers are soft and the sausage is brown. In a bowl mix the remaining stuffing ingredients with the sauteed ingredients and when the stock has flavor, moisten the dressing with it. Do not make too moist, for the bird should be stuffed loosely. Taste for sage flavor.

For The Turkey: Rub the turkey inside and out with lemon juice, then salt and pepper it. Stuff the bird, both cavity and neck-breast area, sew up cavity and rub the turkey all over with softened butter. Put turkey on a rack in a shallow roasting pan, cover with a loose foil tent and roast at 350°, basting with pan fat and wine for 2 to 3 hours until tender. (Since this game bird is not fat like a domestic "butterball" turkey, do not overcook lest you dry it out. Use a meat thermometer and consider it done at 180°. For timing the roasting, consider 18 to 20 minutes to the pound.)

SWIMMIN'

THINGS

Index

Stewed Eel

1½-3 lbs. eel
1½ qts. water
6 T. vinegar
4 cloves
2 tsp. chopped parsley

½ sliced lemon
10 peppercorns
3 bay leaves
½ onion (sliced)

Skin the eel by pulling skin from head to tail in 2-inch sections. Clean each section separately. Pull out membrane and push out intestines with handle of wooden spoon. Rub inside with salt and rinse several times with clean water. Bring the 1½ qts. water and vinegar to boil; scald pieces of eel in water; drain. In saucepan, put eel and remaining ingredients and cover eel with water. Bring to a boil and simmer for 15 minutes; drain. Serve eel with hot butter and lemon juice and wedges.

Baked Eel

Skin eel, split and take back bone out. Cut into 2 to 3 inch pieces. Wash in plenty of salted water. Drain and dry. Dredge in flour, season with paprika, salt, and pepper. Place in greased baking pan. Bake at 400° until brown.

Crayfish

Fresh crayfish
Salt

Pepper
Sauce (optional)

Locate some crayfish or fresh water ''crabs'' as they are sometimes known, in a lake, pond or stream. Take them home alive in a pail or wash tub. Fill the tub or pail with fresh water when you get home and throw in a handful of salt in the water. Leave them in the salty water for 10 minutes. Heat a large kettle of boiling water and add a little salt and pepper to it. When the water is boiling, drop the crayfish alive into the water. Let them boil 3 minutes after they turn a beautiful red color Just like a cooked lobster. Remove them from the water and let them cool. When they are cool, shuck the skin from the tails and you will have the finest shrimp meat. Serve the meat from the tails cold or hot and with any sauce or butter.

(51)

Crawfish Pasta

25-30 large crawfish
1 lb. fine egg noodles
1/8 C. pickling spice
Cheese cloth
4 qts. water
½ lb. butter (or more)

1 clove garlic (crushed) or
* 1 tsp. powder*
1 tsp. parsley flakes
Lemon pepper (to taste)
Bread crumbs (optional)

Place pickling spice in cheese cloth and tie in ball. Put spice ball in water and bring to boil. Drop live crawfish in boiling water. Return to boil and cook for 15 minutes; drain. Shuck meat from shell and set aside. Prepare egg noodles per package directions; drain. Melt water and add garlic, crawfish and lemon pepper. Stir into prepared noodles and parsley flakes. Garnish with bread crumbs. Serve with garlic bread.

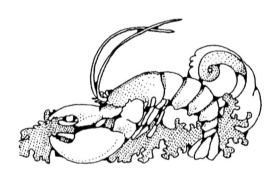

Crawdad Dip

8 crawfish tails (cooked & peeled)
10 ozs. cream cheese
2 T. dry onion soup mix

1 tsp. Worcestershire sauce
2 tsp. lemon juice
¼ tsp. Tabasco sauce

Break crawfish up into tiny pieces. Put all ingredients into bowl. Mix well; chill and serve. Great cracker dip!

Smoked Fish

BRINE:

1 gallon water
4 C. salt
2 C. brown sugar

2 T. crushed black pepper
2 T. crushed bay leaves

Soak fish 2 to 3 hours, depending on size in brine. Remove from brine and rinse with fresh water. Hang in cool shady place for 3 hours or until shiny skin forms on fish. Place in smoker for 4 hours at 110°-120°. Then add dense smoke and raise temperature to 160°-180° for 4 hours.

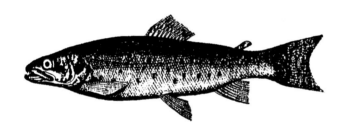

Pickled Fish

7 lbs. fish filets
1 qt. granulated sugar
3 qts. white vinegar

1¾ C. salt
1 box pickling spice
2 medium onions (sliced)

Mix fish and salt in glass container (1 gallon jar works well). Cover with vinegar. Soak for 5 days in refrigerator. Drain and soak in cold water for 1 hour. Wash well and dry. Mix 2 qts. white vinegar, 1 qt. granulated sugar, and 1 box (5 ozs.) pickling spices and heat until sugar is dissolved. Arrange fish and onion slice in 1 gallon jar. Cover with cool solution. Refrigerate for another 5 days.

More Pickled Fish

2-3 lbs. fish (cut into small pieces)   *1 C. salt to 1 qt. water*

Soak in salt brine for 48 hours. Do Not Use metal (use glass or earthen-ware). Boil and cool. Drain, do not rinse. Put fish in clear white vinegar for 48 hours. Drain and pack in hot sterile jars - layer of fish, layer of onion, fish, etc., until jar is full. Make a syrup of:

2 C. vinegar   *1 tsp. whole peppercorns*
1½ C. sugar   *2 tsp. mustard seed*
1 tsp. whole allspice   *1 tsp. whole cloves*

Boil for 5 minutes; cool and pour over fish. Put in 1 bay leaf on top and seal. Keep in refrigerator. (Don't pack too tight.)

Still More Pickled Fish

Fish fillets (cut in bite-size pieces)

FOR EACH QUART OF FISH:
½ C. iodized salt   *1/8 C. Tender Quick Salt*

BRINE - FOR EACH QUART OF FISH:
2 C. vinegar   *1 T. pickling spice*
1 C. sugar   *Onions*

Fillet and take out main bones. Cut into bite-size pieces. For each quart of fish, put fish in jars with salts on top, cover with vinegar and shake well. Refrigerate. Check and shake 2 to 3 times daily for 5 days. On 5th day, drain and rinse well. Let stand in cold water for ½ hour. Make brine while waiting.

For Brine: Combine 2 C. vinegar, 1 C. sugar, and 1 T. pickling spice for each quart of fish. Bring to a boil. Simmer for ½ hour and let cool. Put layer of fish in jar. Next a layer of onions, a layer of fish, a layer of onions, etc., until jar is almost full. Cover with brine. Let stand in refrigerator for 2 to 3 days.

And, Yet Still More Pickled Fish

2 lbs. cut-up fish fillets   *2 C. water*
½ C. canning salt

Cover and let stand in refrigerator for 24 hours. Pour off above liquid. Soak in distilled white vinegar for 24 hours. Pour off above liquid. Cut and chop lots of onion and alternate with packing of fish in jars. Then boil the following mixture:

1 C. white vinegar   *1½ C. sugar*
½ C. water   *2-3 tsp. pickling spice*

Boil and set aside to cool. Then add ½ C. port white wine. Put 10 to 15 whole allspice on top of fish, then pour above liquid mixture over fish. (I usually add a bay leaf to each jar, optional.) Put lids on and keep refrigerated.

Canned Carp

Carp   *Vegetable oil*
Ketchup   *Salt*
Vinegar

Clean fish and cut into chunks. Pack fish into pint jars. Leave at least 1-inch from top of jar. To each pint add 2 T. each of ketchup, vinegar, and oil plus 1 tsp. salt. Seal jars and put in pressure canner at 10 lbs. of pressure for 80 minutes. Bones become soft and fish has salmon taste.

Canned Fish

Per pint cut up fish in 2-inch squares and pack in jars.

ADD:
½ tsp. canning salt   *3 T. vinegar*

Seal and put in pressure cooker for 75 minutes on 10 lbs. pressure. DON'T add any extra water (it will make its own juice). Cool cooker before removing jars.

(55)

Beautiful Golden Fried Bluegills

3 lbs. panfish filets	*2 eggs*
2 C. flour	*1 C. milk*
1 C. cornmeal	

Dry water from fish on paper towels. Mix egg and milk together. Place dried fish in milk-egg mixture. Mix flour and cornmeal together. Roll fish from egg-milk mixture into flour-cornmeal, coating evenly. Deep fat fry until golden brown. Serve with Hoffman House Shrimp Sauce. Serves family of 4.

Microwave Fish

Frozen fish fillets (any kind)	*Onion*
Lemon pepper	*Krazy Mixed-Up Salt*
Butter	*Paprika*

Place fish in microwave casserole. Add layer of onion slices; sprinkle with lemon pepper and Krazy Mixed-Up Salt. Dot with butter and garnish with paprika. Microwave until fish flakes apart.

Good Old Fried Fish

1 lb. fish filets (any kind)	*¼ C. milk*
1 egg	*½ C. corn flake crumbs*
Salt and pepper	*Oil*

Pat fish dry with paper towel. Beat egg well and then add milk, salt, and pepper. Dip fish in egg and milk, then roll in corn flake crumbs. Deep fat fry until golden brown. Use real hot grease.

Mom's Broasted Trout

4 medium pan-sized trout
4-5 slices white bread
4 slices bacon
  (cut into ½-inch pieces)
1 medium onion
  (half chopped, half sliced)
½ tsp. pepper

1 can mushroom slices (drained)
1 large lemon
1 celery rib (chopped fine,
  leaves and all)
½ tsp. savory
½ tsp. salt

Clean, wash, and pat dry the fish, leaving heads and tails on. Fry the bacon until nearly crisp; remove and set aside. Drain off all but about 2 T. of grease. Cook the chopped onion and celery in the bacon drippings until soft but not browned; remove and add to the bacon. Cut bread into cubes and fry in the bacon grease until lightly browned. Remove pan from the flame and add mushrooms, bacon, onions, and celery. Toss lightly with two forks; sprinkle with salt, pepper, and savory; toss again. Stuff trout loosely with this mixture. Prepare two large layered rectangles of aluminum foil. Place thin slices of onion on foil with two trout on top head to tail. Sprinkle with lemonN juice. Fold foil over and seal edges with double fold. Place in a medium-hot oven, 350°-375° and bake for 20 to 25 minutes. Open foil and test for doneness; you may want to cook another 5 to 10 minutes.

Northern Pike Casserole

1 Northern Pike fillets
1 small can diced mushrooms
1 can drained bean sprouts
4 ozs. peas

1 C. skim milk
Salt, pepper & paprika
Mozzarella cheese

Cut fillets into small pieces. Add ingredients in casserole dish and mix together. Sprinkle salt and pepper, to taste. Add mozzarella cheese on top. Sprinkle lightly with paprika after baking for 1 hour at 350°.

Grilled Barbecued Trout

BASTING SAUCE:
½ C. melted butter or margarine   *¼ C. lemon juice*

Trout fillets

Use fresh or thawed trout fillets. Pat fish fillets dry with paper toweling. Brush with salad oil and place on well greased grill. Cook 4-inches from medium-hot coals. Baste frequently while cooking. Grill for 6 minutes on each side. Fish is done when they flake easily with a fork. Sprinkle with salt and pepper.

Baked Cheesie Fish Filets

3 lbs. boneless fish filets   *4 ozs. shredded Cheddar cheese*
1 can cream of mushroom soup   *Pam or similar spray pan coating*
½ can of milk

Preheat oven to 350°. Spray baking pan or cookie sheet with vegetable spray or lightly grease. Lay filets in single layer skin side down and bake until flaky or done. Meanwhile mix mushroom soup and milk in saucepan. Heat until blended. Stir in most of the cheese, reserving some for garnish. Stir until cheese is melted. Remove cooked filets from oven, spoon sauce over top and top with reserved cheese. Serve while hot. Serves approximately 4 to 6 people.

Trout Filets or Steak

2 lbs. trout filets
  or steaks
Salt and pepper

2 T. lemon juice
1 tsp. grated onion
¼ C. butter or margarine (melted)

Heat oven to 350°. If filets are large, cut into serving pieces. Season with salt and pepper. Mix juice, onion, and butter. Dip fish into butter mixture. Place in greased 9x9x2-inch pan. Pour remaining butter mixture over fish. Bake, uncovered for 25 to 30 minutes until fish flakes easily with a fork.

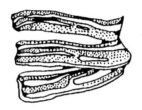

Bass 'N Bacon, Baked

6 medium-sized bass
½ C. cornmeal
1½ tsp. salt

1½ tsp. paprika
6 bacon slices

Clean bass and cut into serving pieces. Mix together cornmeal, salt, and paprika. Dip fish in cornmeal mixture. Place in baking dish. Top with bacon. Bake at 425° for about 20 minutes.

Poor Man's Lobster

2 qts. water
¼-⅓ C. salt
¼ C. vinegar
2 T. dried onion flakes

2 T. dried parsley flakes
1 bay leaf
6-7 large fillets (such as
  walleye, northern, bass, etc.)

Bring water, salt, and vinegar to boil. Add spices and fish. Bring to boil again. Cook until fish are done (about 8 to 10 minutes). Remove from water and put under broiler until dry and crisp (about 3 minutes). Serve with melted butter.

Poached Walleye

3 lbs. walleye (fresh)	*3 T. butter*
2 tsp. salt	*4 T. lemon juice*
1 tsp. pepper	*1 small onion (minced)*
4 T. water	*1 sprig parsley (minced)*

Fillet fish; rub in salt and pepper. Drizzle lemon juice over fillets. Then spread with butter. Sprinkle on onion and parsley. Add water; wrap in foil and place over medium barbecue coals for 20 minutes. Turn occasionally.

Baked Cream Fish

6 fish fillets	*1 can cream of mushroom soup*
1 small onion	*8 ozs. sour cream*
1 can mushroom pieces	*1 C. shredded Cheddar cheese*

Place fish in bottom of baking dish. Cover with chopped mushroom pieces and onions. Bake at 350° for 30 minutes. Drain off liquid. Cover with blended mixture of cream of mushroom soup, sour cream, and shredded cheese. Bake, uncovered for 45 minutes at 350° or until golden brown.

Fish In Foil

1-2 lbs. fish fillets (bluegil,	*Garlic salt*
crappie, perch, bass)	*Onion*
Lawry's seasoning salt	*Butter*

Lay out large piece of foil and place fish in single layer. Season to taste with seasoning salt and garlic salt. Slice onion and separate ring and lay on top of fish. Put pats of butter on top of fish. Fold over the top of fish and foil edges to make a sealed package. Put in oven at 350° for about 45 minutes or this can be cooked on grill in same manner over hot coals for about same time.

Baked Fish

1 whole large snapper or rockfish
Juice of 7 lemons
Water
Dash of hot pepper sauce
2 onions (sliced)

3 tomatoes (sliced)
2 T. butter or margarine
2 T. oil
1¾ C. dry white wine

Place fish in a shallow baking dish and add lemon juice and enough water to cover fish. Sprinkle with hot pepper sauce, cover, and marinate in refrigerator from 2 to 6 hours. Drain marinade, reserving 1 C. of the liquid. Place onions and tomatoes in baking dish and then the fish, dotting with butter and some oil. Add the saved marinade and wine and bake for 30 to 40 minutes at 350°.

Catfish Chowder

5-6 lbs. catfish (skinned & clean)
5-7 potatoes
   (medium, peeled & diced)
1 qt. peeled tomatoes
4 oz. can tomato sauce
1 large onion (chopped)

⅓ lb. butter
½ tsp. thyme
2 T. Worcestershire sauce
Salt (optional)
Pepper, to taste

Place fish in large cook pot and cover with water. Bring to boil. Reduce heat and simmer until fish is well done and flakes. Drain fish, saving liquid, and return it to the pot. Remove bones from fish and return to liquid. Add other ingredients. Cook on low heat to simmer for 1 hour, stirring frequently. Serve hot and enjoy!

Ozark Carp

Use 1 (12-inch) pine board cleaned well. Butter the board all over. Clean carp and place on board. Add salt, pepper, bay leaf, parsley, and thyme, to taste. Bake in moderate oven (350°) for 1hour. When done to a golden brown remove from oven. Carefully remove carp from board, then throw carp away and eat board.

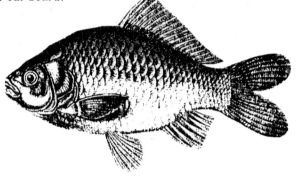

How To Fix Bony Fish

(I've tried this recipe an' there's one durn truble with it. Thet pressure cookin' softens them bones an' they ain't a bit good fer pickin' yore teeth with.)

After fish is dressed, carve cross-wise with a sharp knife. Salt to taste and roll in flour and cornmeal mixed equally. Put in hot fat and fry until brown. put in inset pans and set in pressure cooker with ½-inch of water in bottom of cooker. Cook for 45 minutes with 15 pounds pressure. Fish cooked this way is good warmed over in hot fat in open skillet.

Baked Carp

Choose fresh clear, cold water carp and skin the same as catfish. Cut-up as if to fry. Choose size of roaster to suit amount of fish, then put in a layer of fish rolled in flour with salt and pepper. Then add a layer of bacon strips, then another layer of fish, etc., topping with a layer of smoked bacon strips. Bake and serve warm.

Catfish Soup

2 to 3 lbs. catfish (cut-up)
2 qts. cold water
1 sliced onion
1 chopped celery stalk

Herbs (bay leaf, parsley, thyme)
Salt and pepper
1 C. milk
2 T. butter or fat

Place all ingredients into stew pan and put on slow fire. Stir occasionally and cook until fish is ready to fall to pieces. Serve hot.

Hush Puppies

2 C. cornmeal
½ C. water
1½ C. milk

2 tsp. baking powder
1 tsp. salt
1 medium onion (diced)

Mix all ingredients and drop by teaspoonfuls into very hot deep fat. Fry until golden brown.

Ozark Catfish Balls

Bake or steam catfish. (Modern method is to cook in a pressure cooker.) Remove fish from bones and flake. To every 2 C. flaked fish add 2 T. mashed potatoes, 1 egg, salt, and pepper, to taste. Shape in balls and fry in deep fat.

(63)

Fish, Italian Style

6 fish fillets	½ C. Cheddar cheese
1 jar spaghetti sauce	1 tsp. basil
1½ C. mozzarella cheese	1 tsp. parsley flakes

Place fish in baking dish and bake at 375° for 30 minutes. Drain liquid and cover with spaghetti sauce. Sprinkle with basil and parsley. Cover with mozzarella and Cheddar cheese; bake, uncovered for approximately another 30 minutes.

Fried Fish

2 lbs. fish fillets (any fish)	1 T. seasoned salt
2 C. Frying Magic	Oil

Shake Frying Magic and salt together. Throw in fish and shake until coated. Then fry in ½ oil in heavy skillet until done.

Fish Soup

1½ lbs. boneless fish	3 bay leaves
2 cans cream of mushroom soup	6 peppercorns
1 medium onion (diced)	2 C. milk
2 C. potatoes (cubed)	5 pats butter

Put potatoes, onion, bay leaves, and peppercorn in pot and cover with water. Boil until potatoes are tender. Add fish and boil at medium heat for ½ hour. Add soup and simmer for ½ hour. Heat milk in separate pan, then add to soup (milk will curdle if added cold). Add butter before serving, salt and pepper, to taste.

Frog Legs

Skin the froglegs, wash, and cut off feet. Soak at least 1 hour in salt water. Lightly beat egg. Season legs with salt and pepper. Dip in cornmeal (or bread crumbs), then in egg and again in cornmeal. Fry in deep hot fat. Drain fat before serving.

Pan Fried Fish

(Lawsey! Thars jest nothin' better th'n fresh caught fish. Pa was always real good, after spendin' all day catchin' th fish, to hurry them home so's I culd git them scaled an' cleaned real soon fer his supper. He shore is nice thataway.)

Scale and clean fish well, and wash very good in cold water. If small, fry them as is. If large, cross-slit them along side so they cook better. Salt them and then roll in flour and meal mixed equally. Fry in ½ to 1-inch of hot fat. Turn and brown on both sides. Serve hot.

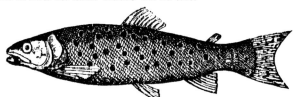

Snapping Turtle Stew

2 lbs. prepared turtle meat	3 medium potatoes (diced)
Butter	1 small can tomatoes
Water for stew	3 medium sized carrots
1 medium onion	½ C. chopped parsley
2 C. celery	Salt
1 C. lima beans (soaked)	Pepper

Cut meat in 1-inch pieces. Melt a generous amount of butter in frying pan and brown meat on all sides; remove from heat. Bring water for stew to boil. Add onion, celery, and beans; simmer for ½ hour. Add all ingredients. Cook slowly for 45 minutes.

Salmon Potatoes

6 medium baking potatoes	1 T. lemon juice
⅓ C. milk	2 T. butter
1 egg (beaten)	1½ C. salmon
1 tsp. salt	⅓ C. minced onion
½ tsp. paprika	Buttered bread crumbs

Bake potatoes. Saute' salmon and onions in butter. Split potatoes and scoop out inside and mix with milk, egg, salt, paprika, lemon juice, sauteed salmon, and onions. Return to shell and bake at 325° for 25 minutes. Sprinkle with bread crumbs.

Salmon Salad

2 C. cooked (leftover) salmon	½ C. chopped celery
3 hard-boiled eggs	¼ head lettuce (shredded)
Salt and pepper	½ green pepper (chopped)
¼ tsp. Italian seasoning	½ onion (diced)

Fish Cakes

1 small onion (chopped fine)	½ tsp. salt
2 T. shortening	¼ tsp. black pepper
1½ C. cooked fish	1 T. dried egg
3 C. diced, boiled potatoes	½ C. water

Fry the onion in a small amount of shortening until soft. Then mix with fish, potatoes, and seasoning. Stir the egg in the water. Add this and the remainder of shortening to the other ingredients. Form into small cakes ¾-inch thick and fry in a greased pan until brown.

Beer Batter for Fish

1 C. flour
½ tsp. sugar
½ tsp. salt

1 egg
1 C. cold beer
2 T. oil

Beat ingredients. Dip fish in batter and fry in hot oil (375°) until golden brown. Drain on paper towels.

Fish Batter

¼ C. cornstarch
¼ C. beer
2 eggs (separated)

¼ C. flour
Pinch of salt
Pinch of sugar

Mix beer in egg yolks and add the rest of the ingredients. Beat egg whites until stiff. Fold stiffly beaten egg whites into the egg yolk mixture. Dip fish into this batter and fry until golden brown.

Fried Frog Legs

Clean legs and soak in salt water. A small amount of lemon juice may be added for a little tang to meat. Roll in seasoned flour or your favorite fish breading and fry until golden brown in deep fat at 375°.

Turtle Soup

·2 lbs. turtle
1 large onion (chopped)
2 large potatoes (diced)
1½ C. celery (chopped)

2 carrots (sliced or cut)
1 qt. Half and Half
¼ lb. butter

Boil turtle with onion using only enough water to cover turtle. Remove meat from bones and return it to the broth. In separate pan boil the potatoes, celery, and carrots. Drain and add to turtle and onion broth. Warm the Half and Half the the butter until blended. Add this to the other ingredients. Season and simmer to desired thickness. May want to add some milk to thin.

Turtle Stew

2 lbs. turtle meat (cut-up)
2 bay leaves
1 stalk celery
½ small onion (cut-up)
1 T. chopped parsley
2 tsp. vinegar

Pepper
2 tsp. salt
3 T. bacon drippings or
   chicken fat
½ C. canned milk or
   Half & Half

THICKENING:
2 T. flour
1 tsp. Worcestershire sauce

Water to make paste

Combine in kettle the first 8 ingredients and add water to cover meat. Cover and boil until tender. When tender add the 2 tsp. vinegar to liquid and the thickening. Gradually add the milk. Stir slowly into simmering liquid and meat. Cook for 3 minutes, stirring constantly. Season to taste.

White Stew of Terrapin

Cut off heads and soak in cold water to draw out blood. Scald terrapins to loosen skin and nails. Cover with water and boil with a small onion chopped fine, parsley and thyme. When done the shell will come loose easily. Remove meat, including liver and any eggs; chop fine and return to the pot. Rub 1 T. flour into butter the size of a hen's egg; stir into stock, adding salt and red pepper, to taste. Just before serving add a coffee-cup full of sweet cream and a bit of wine, if desired.

Turtle Soup

1½ qt. strained chicken broth
1 lb. turtle meat (without bone)
3 T. chicken fat
1 medium onion (chopped)

Salt and pepper, to taste
1 T. chopped parsley
5-6 thin slices lemon

Prepare a richly flavored chicken broth seasoned only with salt; strain. Cut turtle meat into small pieces. Brown slowly in the chicken fat (or butter). Add onion and saute' slowly over medium heat until soft and yellow. Add turtle, seasoning, and any fat to chicken broth; heat to boiling. Reduce heat and simmer gently for 10 minutes. Serve with a sprinkling of parsley on each bowl of soup and a paper-thin slice of lemon floated on top. Serves 5 to 6.

Fried Turtle

To fry turtle it is advised to parboil or cook in pressure cooker until tender first. Then roll in flour or meal and seasonings. Fry in deep fat.

Snappin' Turtle

Success of preparing turtle to eat depends a great deal on proper dressing. To dress a snapping turtle, scrub all mud an dirt from him and then cut off head and toes. With a spike nail, secure turtle to a large plant or slab, breast up, by piercing center of the breast bone. With a sharp knife cut skin loose from shell around 1 front leg, then the other, separating in two pieces at the neck. Then pull the skin off 1 egg, then the other. This can be done more easily with 2 persons working together, 1 at each end pulling against each other. Start with the right front leg and left hind leg, then grasp both legs and neck in one hand and insert the point of a stout knife at base of neck bone and giving a twist until the legs and neck come loose. Use same procedure on hind legs and tail. Remove breast bone, spike, and entrails. Then with a sharp hatchet or cleaver chop along tenderloin on each side, then trim top shell loose. Trim all of water fat from meat and discard. Rinse and meat is ready to use in any of the following recipes.

Stewed Terrapin
(Use Four Terrapins)

The terrapins must be alive. Plunge the terrapins alive into boiling water and let them remain until the sides and lower shell begin to crack — this will take less than an hour; then remove them and let them get cold. Take off the shell and outer skin, being careful to save all the blood possible in opening them. If there are eggs in them put them aside in a dish; take all the inside out, and be very careful not to break the gall, which must be immediately removed or it will make the rest bitter. It lies within the liver. Then cut-up the liver and all the rest of the terrapin into small pieces, adding the blood and juice that have flowed out in cuttin up. Add ½ pt. of water and sprinkle a little flour over them as you place them in the stewpan. Let them stew slowly for 10 minutes, adding salt, black, and cayenne pepper, and a very small blade of mace. Then add a gill of the best brandy and ½ pt. of the very best sherry wine; then let simmer over a slow fire very gently. In about 10 minutes or so, before you are ready to dish them, add half a pint of rich cream, and ½ lb. of sweet butter with flour to prevent boiling. 2 or 3 minutes before taking them off the fire, peel the eggs carefully and throw them in whole. If there should be no eggs use the yolks of hen eggs (hard-boiled). Serve warm.

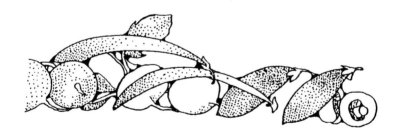

Turtle Soup or Stew

A delicious soup can be prepared the same as with a choice piece of beef or pork. A delicious stew can be made the same by adding the desired vegetables.

More Turtle Soup

1-2 lbs. meat
Flour & water thickening mixture
Milk and Half & Half

1 onion (sliced)
⅓ C. pickling spices
Salt, to taste

Cover meat with water. Tie onion and pickling spices in cloth bag and add to water. Cook until meat falls from bones; add salt. Remove meat and spice bag. Thicken broth with mixture of flour and water; add milk and Half & Half to thickened broth. Add meat that has been removed from bones. Heat well but don't boil!

Turtle and Rice Casserole

3 lbs. turtle
1 can Cheddar cheese soup
1 C. flour

Uncle Ben's wild rice mix
2 small cans mushrooms
¼ C. oil

Cook wild rice mix per directions. Coat turtle with flour and fry in oil. In a casserole dish add cooked rice mix, Cheddar cheese soup, mushrooms, and fried turtle. Stir together. Cover dish and bake at 350° for 30 to 40 minutes.

Aunt Sue's Fried Turtle

Cut turtle in small pieces. Roll or shake in flour seasoned with salt and pepper and fry until golden brown in skillet. Place pieces on rack in a roaster and cover with sliced onions and drippings from frying. Add a small amount of water for steam and put in a slow oven (300°) for at least 2 hours or until tender. Extremely delicious!

Turtle Stew

3 lbs. turtle meat
4 qts. water
2 onions (chopped)
2 stalks celery (chopped fine)
1 tsp. pickling spices
3 T. butter

1 T. salt
1 tsp. sugar
1 C. tomatoes
½ tsp. black pepper
1 tsp. parsley (chopped)

Place turtle in large kettle with water, salt, and pepper. Tie onion, celery, parsley, and pickling spices in bag and place in kettle with turtle. Bring to a boil and simmer until the turtle meat falls apart. Remove the vegetable and spice bag. Add tomatoes, butter, and sugar. Heat until very hot, and serve.

Stewed Turtle

2-3 lbs. turtle meat
1 onion (cut-up)
1 tsp. mixed pickling spice
   (tied in bag)
Flour

½ tsp. vinegar
2 tsp. salt
¼ tsp. black pepper
Half & Half

Place turtle in large kettle and cover with water. Add onion, salt, pepper, and the spice bag. Cook turtle until it is tender and falls apart. Remove the turtle from broth, remove spice bag. Thicken the broth with flour like gravy; add about 1 C. of Half & Half or cream may be used, to the soup; add turtle meat and heat just to hot (do not overcook after cream has been added). More vinegar may be added according to taste. Serves 4 to 6.

(73)

Real Good Clam Chowder

¼ lb. salt pork or bacon (cubed)
2 small onions (minced)
8-10 ozs. clams or clam meat
6-8 medium potatoes (cubed)

Salt and pepper, to taste
1 can evaporated milk
2 C. Half & Half cream

Fry salt pork or bacon until brown. Add onions and cook until tender. Add cubed potatoes and enough water to cook. Add clams. Cook until potatoes are tender. Add seasonings, evaporated milk, and Half & Half; heat well. Serve with crackers. Serves 8.

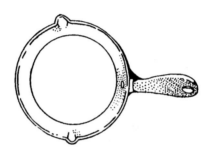

Jus' Plain Clam Chowder

¼ lb. salt pork (may use bacon)
2 large onions (chopped)
1 carrot (diced)
2 C. cooked tomatoes
1 green pepper (diced)
1 C. diced celery

4 C. water
¼ tsp. thyme
White pepper & salt, to taste
1 dozen clams or 1 (10½ oz.)
  canned clams
1 C. diced potatoes

Dice salt pork, brown and remove cracklings from fat. Brown onions, carrot, celery, green pepper, and potatoes in fat. Add tomatoes, water, and seasonings. Cook for 10 minutes. Add clams and liquid. Simmer until all is tender; thicken with crushed soda crackers to desired thickness. Serves 6.

Seashore Clam Chowder

3 C. chicken broth
1/3 C. diced celery
1 carrot (diced)
1 dozen fresh clams or
  1 (10½ oz.) can clams
3 T. butter

2 C. diced raw, peeled potatoes
2 T. chopped onion
2 T. flour
½ C. Half & Half
Salt and pepper, to taste

Steam fresh clams and pry open. Drain off and measure liquid so you have 1 cup. Put carrots, potatoes, and celery into chicken broth. Cover and cook slowly until tender. Then saute' clams and onions in butter for 5 minutes to just light brown. Blend flour evenly into the mixture. Add broth and vegetables gradually, stirring to keep smooth. Add clam broth, cream, and seasonings. Reheat just to boiling and serve. Makes 8 cups.

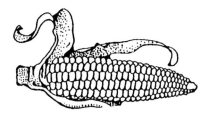

Corned Clam Casserole

3 eggs (beaten)
1 T. minced onion
1 C. cream-style corn
1 (7 oz.) can clam
½ tsp. chopped parsley
½ C. croutons

1 T. butter
1½ T. diced pimientos
Dash of cayenne pepper
Salt and pepper, to taste
Milk

Drain liquid from clam and add enough milk to make 1 cup. Combine with beaten eggs. Add all remaining ingredients and pour into greased casserole. Bake at 375° until set firm, about 45 minutes. Serves 6.

Clambake

25 clams
4-6 ears corn (wrapped in foil)
4-6 potatoes (wrapped in foil)
1 chicken (wrapped in
   cheesecloth & tied)
   (cut in serving pieces)

Juice of 1 lemon
1 qt. water
1 tsp. salt
¼ tsp. pepper
1 T. chopped parsley

In large enamel pot, add water, salt, pepper, parsley, and lemon juice; bring to a boil. Add potatoes, cover, and cook for 15 minutes. Add the chicken, cover, and cook for 20 minutes. Turn chicken and cook for 10 minutes. Add corn and cook for 10 for minutes. Add clams and cook and steam until clams open. Serve with melted butter and clam juice.

Clams on The Beach

24 clams
Foil
Butter

Charcoal
Salt and pepper

Dig a hole 18-inches deep and wide enough to hold the clams. Make a bed of coals and cover with 5-inches of sand. Place foil on sand, line the clams on the foil and cover with foil. Cover the foil with sand and let bake for 1 hour. Serve with melted butter.

Scalloped Clams

1½ C. minced clams or
   canned clams
2 T. minced onions
½ C. butter
½ C. bread crumbs or
   cracker crumbs

Salt and white pepper, to taste
2 T. chopped parsley
⅓ C. milk
¼ tsp. lemon
¼ tsp. paprika

Melt butter; add crumbs, salt, pepper, parsley, and paprika. Mix, reserving ⅓ for topping. Mix remainder with clams, milk, lemon juice, and onions. Pour in oiled casserole. Sprinkle with crumbs and dot with butter. Bake at 375°, uncovered for 25 minutes.

Clams 'N Toast

1 C. minced clams
1 C. milk
2 T. flour
2 T. butter

1 tsp. chives
1 C. Half & Half milk
1/8 tsp. red pepper
¼ tsp. salt

In saucepan, blend flour and butter. Meanwhile, bring milk to a boil; add all at once to flour mixture, stirring until smooth. Add chives, cream, and other seasonings. Serve hot on toast.

For Cryin' Out Loud
Fried Turtle and Onions

1 turtle (cut in serving pieces)
1 C. flour
3 T. oil
1 tsp. salt

3-4 onions (sliced)
1 clove garlic (crushed) (if desired)
Pepper, to taste
½ tsp. caraway seed

Dredge the turtle in seasoned flour. Fry to brown on all sides in hot oil. Sprinkle with caraway seeds, onion, and garlic. Add 1 C. of water; cover and simmer for 1 hour or until tender and water has cooked away.

Turtle Soup

2 lbs. turtle meat (cooked)   1 T. chopped parsley
2 qts. chicken stock (strained)   5 thin slices of lemon
1 onion (sliced)   Salt and pepper, to taste
3 T. oil

Brown turtle in oil. Add sliced onions and saute' till just tender not brown. Add turtle, onion, salt, and pepper to hot chicken stock; heat to boiling and add parsley and simmer for 25 minutes. Serve hot.

Baked Turtle Steaks

1 turtle steak   ¼ tsp. curry powder
1 (4 oz.) can mushrooms (drained)   Salt and pepper, to taste
1 pkg. brown gravy mix   Parmesan cheese
2 T. oil

Brown turtle steaks in oil to just brown. Place steaks in baking dish according to the amount of meat. Mix brown gravy mix according to package directions. Season turtle with curry powder, salt, and pepper. Add drained mushrooms and gravy mix. Cover and bake at 325° for 1 hour or when meat is tested and is tender. Sprinkle with Parmesan cheese and return To 350° oven, uncovered for 10 minutes, until cheese melts and is bubbly. Serve with hot rice.

Fried Turtle

5 lbs. turtle meat   4 large onions (optional)
Pinch of caraway   2 garlic cloves (minced) (optional)
½ tsp. salt   1 C. flour
½ C. water   2 T. oil

Dredge turtle in flour. When oil is hot, add turtle and brown. Add onion, caraway, garlic, salt, pepper, and water. Heat slowly for 1 hour. When most of water is gone, increase heat and fry for 1 hour.

Another Turtle Stew

1 turtle (cut in pieces)
1 large onion (cut-up)
1 tsp. mixed pickling spices
   (tied in bag)

½ tsp. vinegar
3 T. flour
2 C. milk

Combine all ingredients in large kettle, except flour and milk. Fill kettle with as much water as you'll want for soup and enough to cover the turtle. Cover and boil until tender, will take a couple of hours. Pour through a strainer and put juice and meat back in kettle. Take spice bag out after cooking with turtle for 1 hour. Make a thickening of flour and 1 C. of milk. Add to turtle and juice slowly and add rest of milk. Heat but do not boil.

Fried Frog Legs

¼ C. butter or margarine
2 lbs. frog legs
Salt and white pepper, to taste

¼ C. flour or cornmeal
   (may mix both together)
1 tsp. grated onion

Dry legs with paper towel. Mix salt, pepper, and flour mixture; coat frog legs. Fry in hot butter until browned, add onion for 5 minutes before frog legs are done and browned. Cover and cook for 15 to 18 minutes more or until tender. Serve hot. Serves 3 to 5.

Frog Legs

½ lb. sliced mushrooms
2 slices eggplant (diced)
2½ lbs. fresh frog legs
   (don't soak in water)

2 garlic cloves
1 C. tomatoes
1 lemon, juice
2 T. butter

Saute' the frog legs and garlic in butter. Season with salt and pepper. Remove garlic; add eggplant, mushrooms, and tomatoes. Add juice of 1 lemon. Simmer until tender. Serves 3 to 6.

Tipsy Frog Legs

PART I:
1 lb. frog legs
1 leek or small onion
4 T. butter
4 T. white wine
Salt and pepper

1½ qts. water
2 T. parsley
½ C. chopped celery
2 carrots (diced)
Thyme

PART II:
1 T. minced onion
2 T. butter
1½ C. long grained
   uncooked rice

Liquid from Part I
½ C. butter
3½ ozs. Parmesan cheese

Brown leek or onion in butter; add frog legs and fry. Add wine and cook until liquid has evaporated. Remove frog legs and set aside, then add liquid and seasoning to pan. Boil for 30 minutes. Use broth from Part II.

For Part II: Brown onion in butter; add rice and mix well. Add broth and cook very slowly until rice is tender. Remove from fire and fold in butter, cheese, and frog legs; salt and pepper, to taste.

LITTLE CRITTERS

THAT SNEAK

AROUND

IN THE WOODS

Index

All About Small Game

The rule of punctual field care applies to small game. Immediate dressing of small game will delay spoilage caused by body heat and bacteria. Fortunately, it is easier to eviscerate and skin game animals while still wram.

After removing skin, cut animal open down the stomach, being sure to break the bone behind the hind legs. Clean the inside, then wipe the carcass thoroughly with a clean dry cloth or dry leaves.

Keep the catch cool and transport in the open air or in a ventilated car. When at home, soak meat in cold water and keep refrigerated. If not used within 24 hours, freeze in plastic bags.

Roast Squirrels

3 squirrels
¾ C. oil
¼ C. lemon juice
2 C. bread crumbs
½ C. Half & Half

1 C. sauteed mushrooms
½ tsp. salt
¼ tsp. pepper
¼ C. finely chopped onions
4 T. olive oil

Dress and clean squirrels. Soak in cold water about 1 hour. Dry off squirrels. Cover with oil and lemon juice. Let stand for 1 hour. Combine crumbs with just enough milk to moisten, mushrooms, salt, pepper, and onions. Stuff squirrels with this mixture. Put in roaster, brush with olive oil. Roast uncovered at 325° for 1½-2 hours until tender. Baste every 15 minutes. Good served with pan gravy. Serves 6.

Ground Hog

When ground hog is dressed be sure to remove the kernel from under the front legs to keep from making it taste. Cut-up and salt, to taste. Roll in flour, put in hot fat, and fry until brown. Then put in inset pans in pressure cooker with ½-inch water in bottom of cooker. Cook for 70 minutes with 15 pounds of pressure. Possum can be cooked the same way with good results.

Muskrat Maryland

1 large muskrat (1½-2 lbs.)
1 qt. water
1½ tsp. salt
1 small onion (diced)
½ tsp. poultry seasoning
1 egg

½ C. milk
¾ C. flour
1 tsp. salt
¼ tsp. thyme
⅓ C. shortening
Water

Wipe muskrat with damp cloth; pick off any hair. Separate hind from fore quarters, cutting across the back and just below ribs. Put in glass bowl. Add salt water to cover (1 tsp. to 1 qt. water). Cover and place in refrigerator overnight. Drain and rinse with clear water. Place in pan. Add water, salt, onion, and poultry seasoning. Heat to boiling and reduce heat. Cover and simmer for 20 minutes. Remove meat, drain, and cut in serving pieces. Make a batter of egg, milk, and flour. Add salt and thyme. Dip meat in batter and brown slowly in shortening. Add ¼ C. water, cover, and simmer for 20 minutes. Remove cover and cook for 15 to 20 minutes until crisp. Good served with cream gravy.

Baked Squirrel

4 squirrels (cut-up)
Flour
1 can bouillon
¼ C. Worcestershire sauce
2 T. chopped parsley

2 T. onion juice
1 clove garlic
1 small bay leaf
Salt and pepper

Dredge squirrels with flour and brown in roasting pan. Add remaining ingredients. Bake at 350° for 45 minutes. Reduce heat and bake slowly until tender. Serves 4 to 6.

*"I know this doesn't look like a lot of squirrels.
But ours look like this ever since the nuke plant
moved in next door."*

Squirrel Fricassee

1 young squirrel (cut in pieces)
½ C. flour
½ tsp. salt
1/8 tsp. pepper

3 slices bacon (cubed)
¼ C. onion (chopped)
10½ oz. can chicken broth

Mix flour, salt, and pepper in bowl. Coat squirrel with mixture. Fry bacon until grease begins to collect. Add meat and fry until well browned. Add onion and broth. Cover and reduce heat to low. Cook for 2 to 2½ hours or until tender. If desired, make gravy from pan drippings just before serving.

Sour Cream Squirrel

2-3 squirrels (minus rib sections)
1 large onion
Salt
Pepper

3-6 bay leaves
1 C. Half & Half
Cornstarch
Vinegar

Bring squirrel to boil and simmer until tender with salt, pepper, onion, and bay leaves. Have enough water to make a gravy. When tender, add Half & Half. Then thicken with cornstarch. Absolutely last - add vinegar to taste, approximately 3 T. or more.

Game and Rice Casserole

1 C. chopped celery
½ C. chopped onion
¼ C. chopped green pepper
1 (4 oz.) can mushrooms

2 C. wild or brown rice
2 C. liquid (milk, broth)
Rabbit or pheasant pieces

Place celery, onion, green pepper, and mushrooms in 9x13-inch casserole dish. Sprinkle with rice. Pour on liquid. Layer meat pieces. Cover with foil and bake at 325° for about 2 hours.

Squirrels

Young tender squirrels can be fried, broiled, and roasted. Older squirrels need to be simmered, fricasseed, or braised. Remove the scent glands in the small of the back and under the forelegs and the thighs. These should be removed without cutting them, after skinning and squirrel has been drawn. Wash the squirrel and wipe dry to remove any fur that clings to the skin. Soak the cleaned squirrel in a solution of 1 T. of salt to 1 qt. of water for 3 hours. Rinse in cold water and drain.

Sweet Potatoes 'N Squirrel

3 small squirrels
(cut-up in pieces)
½ C. flour
2 T. oil
1 C. water

2 sweet potatoes
(peeled, cut in halves)
Salt and pepper, to taste
1 T. lemon juice

Dredge squirrel in flour. Salt and pepper, to taste. Brown in hot oil and place browned squirrel in greased roaster. Add water and lemon juice. Bake at 350° for 1¼ hours, basting every 15 minutes. Place sweet potatoes around squirrel and bake 30 more minutes or until squirrel and sweet potatoes are tender. Serves 4 to 5. Note: White potatoes may be used in place of sweet and add 1 C. sliced onions to squirrel the last 30 minutes or roasting.

Broiled Squirrel

Place cleaned squirrel on hot broiling rack that has been brushed with butter and sprinkled with salt and pepper. Broil for about 40 minutes, turning frequently and basting with drippings every 10 minutes. Serve with lemon wedges.

Fire Department
Squirrel Stew

6½ gals. water
60-65 cleaned squirrels
3 stewing hens (cut-up)
3 lbs. salt pork (chopped)
2 cloves garlic (chopped)
1 large onion (chopped)
2 gals. lima beans
3 T. parsley
1¼ C. sugar (more can be added)
4 gals. tomatoes

1 gal. carrots (sliced)
2 gals. cut corn
1 gal. green string beans (cut)
1 gal. shredded cabbage
1 tsp. red pepper
¼ C. lemon juice
1 C. salt
¼ C. black pepper
3½ gals. chopped, peeled potatoes
6 T. beef or chicken base

Cut-up the squirrels and chickens in servings that have been cleaned and washed. Bring 4 gallons water to boiling; add squirrels and chickens. Cook until tender, debone. Chop and fry salt pork; drain. Add all other ingredients, except cabbage; cook until tender. Add cabbage and seasonings; simmer for 1 hour. Makes 15 to 17 gallons, depending on how much water you add. Serves about 5 tons of hungry firemen.

Fried Squirrel

2 dressed, cleaned squirrels
½ C. flour
1 tsp. paprika

¼ C. cooking oil
Salt and pepper, to taste
Water, if needed

Wash squirrels and cut in serving pieces. Cover with salted water, that ¼ C. vinegar has been added; let stand for 8 hours, then drain. If rabbit is old, parboil for 10 minutes; drain. Dredge in flour, paprika, salt, and pepper. Fry in cooking oil until tender. Serves 3 to 4. Note: Sliced onions may be added the last 15 minutes of cooking time.

(86)

Baked Squirrel

3 squirrels, cleaned & cut in serving pieces

¼ C. flour
2 T. oil
1 onion (chopped)
1 can cream of mushroom soup

1 (4 oz.) can mushrooms
½ C. or milk
*   more water may be added)*

Clean and wash squirrels; cover with water that salt and vinegar have been added; soak overnight. Drain and dry. Dredge in seasoned flour and brown in oil. Place in roaster. Mix soup and milk. Sprinkle onion around squirrels. Pour soup mixture over squirrels. Cover and bake at 325° for 1 hour. Add mushrooms and continue baking for 30 minute or until squirrels are tender. Serve with rice or potatoes. Serves 4 to 6.

Squirrel and Mushrooms Dressing

4 small squirrels
¾ C. cooking oil
¼ C. lemon juice
2 C. bread crumbs
½ C. of Half & Half
4 T. bacon drippings

¼ C. chopped onion
1 (4 oz.) can mushrooms
Salt and pepper, to taste
1 T. chopped parsley
½ C. water

Cover cleaned squirrels with cooking oil that ¼ C. of vinegar has been added; let stand overnight, in cold place (3 to 4 hours if in a hurry). Combine crumbs with the ½ and ½, mushrooms, onions, salt, and pepper. Stuff squirrels with mixture and sew and truss. Brush with bacon drippings. Mix water and lemon juice together; pour around squirrels. Bake at 325° for 1½ to 2 hours, uncovered. Baste every 15 to 20 minutes. Serves 6 to 8.

Squirrels and Vegetables

3 squirrels
1 lb. carrots
1 C. celery (cut in cubes)
6 T. fat or less
6 T. flour

3 medium potatoes
  (cubed in large chunks)
1 onion (chopped)
Salt and pepper, to taste
½ C. red wine

Clean the squirrels, cut in halves lenthwise, simmer in water to cover with salt and pepper. Cook until squirrels are tender. Remove from borth; add vegetables to broth and simmer until they are just tender. Blend 6 T. flour and 6 T. fat to the broth and vegetables; simmer for 5 minutes. Add wine and squirrels. Serves 6. Keep squirrels hot, if desired and serve vegetables around the cooked squirrels instead of putting squirrels in vegetables.

Muskrat Patties

Remove glands and clean muskrat well. Remove meat from bones and grind. Add onion, salt, pepper, bread crumbs, egg, and fat; mix thoroughly. Form 3-inch into patties. Dip into egg and then in bread crumbs. Fry until brown in hot fat. Cover with jelly sauce and bake in slow oven for 1 hour.

Muskrat Fricassee

1 qt. water	¼ C. shortening
1 dressed muskrat, 1-1½ lb.)	¾ C. water
¼ C. flour	1/16 tsp. red pepper
1 T. salt	1 large onion (sliced)
¼ tsp. pepper	2 tsp. salt

(Note: Be sure to remove all glands from muskrat before cooking. These glands lie under the body and are light yellow. Also between the forelegs, between the shoulders, back and under the thighs. Cut these out carefully.)

With damp cloth, wipe muskrat, pick off hair, cut across back and below ribs. Put in glass or enamel bowl, add salt and water to cover. Refrigerate overnight. Drain and rinse muskrat in clear water. Cut in pieces and roll in peppers, salt, and flour. Place coated pieces in heavy skillet; brown slowly. Sprinkle the brown pieces with paprika. Add onion, cooked until slightly yellow and transparent. Add ½ C. water and simmer for 20 to 30 minutes. May need to add more water. Makes 2 to 3 servings.

Fried Muskrat

1 qt. water	1 egg
1 large dressed muskrat	1 tsp. salt
1 onion (large)	¼ tsp. thyme
½ tsp. poultry seasoning	¾ C. flour
1½ tsp. salt	⅓ C. shortening
½ C. milk	Water

With damp cloth, wipe muskrat clean of hair. Cut across back and below the ribs. Put into glass or enamel bowl. Cover with salt water (1 T. salt to 1 qt. water). Refrgerate overnight. Drain and rinse in clear water. Place in kettle and add water, salt, poultry seasoning, and onion; simmer for 20 minutes. Remove parboiled muskrat, cut into serving pieces. Beat flour, milk, and eggs; add salt and thyme. Dip muskrat in batter and brown slowly. Add ¼ C. water, cover, and simmer 20 minutes. Remove, cover, and cook for 15 to 20 minutes until crisp. Makes 2 to 4 servings.

Rabbit

All varieties of rabbits have scent glands that are small, waxy-looking kernels under their forelegs and on either side of the spine in the small of the back by the spine. These should be removed, taking care not to cut them.

To remove the wild flavor from rabbits, marinate in solution of: 1 part vinegar or lemon juice to 3 parts of salad oil and season with any species preferred; dill seed, garlic, onion, thyme, bay leaves, cloves, celery seed are good. This will give milder flavor as well as tenderize meat fibers. This is particularly important if animal is older, for the fibers of such are tough and dry. Marinate 12 hours. For less spicy marinade, use only vinegar or lemon juice and oil and marinate 12 hours.

When buying rabbits: Young rabbits are known as "fryers" and usually weight not less than 1½ lbs. and rarely over 3½ pounds. Rabbits known as "roasters" weigh 4 pounds and over.

More Rabbit

1 (3 lb.) rabbit	¼ C. chopped green pepper
(cut into serving pieces)	1 T. chili powder
½ C. oil	1 C. catsup
½ C. chopped onion	1 C. water
2 T. oil	2 T. brown sugar
½ C. chopped celery	2 T. Worcestershire sauce
¼ C. chopped green pepper	1 tsp. salt

Brown rabbit in ½ C. fat. Cook onion, celery, and green pepper in 2 T. oil until tender. Add remaining ingredients and bring to a boil. Arrange rabbit in a large, flat baking dish. Pour sauce over. Bake, uncovered at 350° for 30 minutes. Turn rabbit pieces and bake until tender. Serves 4 to 5.

Oven Fried Rabbit

1 rabbit (cut into pieces)
1 C. flour
1 T. paprika
1⅓ tsp. salt

¼ C. melted margarine
¼ C. melted shortening
½ C. water
Black pepper

Mix flour and paprika. Roll rabbit in mixture. Salt and pepper. Place in a greased roaster. Pour melted margarine and shortening over rabbit. Cover and bake at 350° for 2 hours. At the end of 45 minutes, turn each piece and add water. Note: After rabbit has been baking 45 minutes, add 1 medium onion (sliced thin) and continue baking until done. For a tangier taste to the rabbit. Serves 4.

Rabbit with Sour Cream Gravy

1 rabbit (cut in serving pieces)
2 T. oil
2 onions (chopped)
2 C. sour cream
   (dairy sour cream)
2 slices lemon

½ tsp. crushed oregano
1 bay leaf
3 T. wine vinegar
½ tsp. sugar
1½ T. flour

Season rabbit with salt. Dredge rabbit in flour. Put rabbit in hot skillet with oil. Brown rabbit and add 2 chopped onions, 2 slices lemon, ½ tsp. crushed oregano, 1 bay leaf, and black pepper, to taste. Add vinegar and let it steam or simmer until tender. Remove rabbit from skillet. Put 1 T. butter in skillet with 1½ T. flour. Mix well and add 2 C. thick sour cream (dairy sour cream). Bring just to boil and season to taste. Remove bay leaf. If too thick, add a little water. Pour over rabbit and serve with boiled potatoes. Serves 5.

Curried Rabbit

4 lbs. rabbit (cut in serving pieces)	2 T. water
2 T. curry powder	1 tsp. vinegar
4 T. fat	1¼ tsp. cornstarch
2 chopped onions	1 C. water
2½ tsp. salt	

Melt fat and brown rabbit well. Combine salt and curry powder; season rabbit. Add water, vinegar, and onions. Cover tightly and cook until tender. Remove rabbit. Thicken gravy with cornstarch and water paste. Goes good with rice.

Hassenpfeffer

Dress rabbit and wash carefully. Cut in serving pieces. Place in stone crock with equal parts water and vinegar, 3 T. pickling salt, 1 T. pickling spice, and 2 tsp. pepper, and 4 large sliced onions has been added to each 1 gallon of water. Place small plate on top and weight down. Let stand 2 days. Take rabbit out of brine; place rabbit in roaster and add enough liquid from crock to cover rabbit pieces. Bake at 350° until rabbit is tender, 30 minutes before rabbit is done, strain onions from crock and place on rabbit. When rabbit is tender, take out of roaster and debone. To the liquid add 1 tsp. cinnamon, ¼ tsp. cloves, ½ tsp. allspice, 1 additional onion (chopped), and juice from 1 lemon. Thicken with flour to desired thickness and simmer for 4 minutes. Add deboned rabbit and simmer for 35 minutes. Serve hot over boiled potatoes with jackets on.

"I have no idea what kind of critter this is, but its a picture about the right size for this space."

BBQ Rabbit

Cut up a 3 lb. rabbit, salt, and pepper. Brown floured rabbit in small amount of shortening. Pour off any excess fat. Put in roaster and pour sauce over it.

SAUCE:

1 small onion (chopped)	1/8 tsp. cayenne pepper
2 T. butter or margarine	½ tsp. dry or prepared mustard
2 T. brown sugar	½ tsp. chili powder
2 T. vinegar	1 C. tomato catsup
½ tsp. salt	1 tsp. paprika
2 T. lemon juice	2 tsp. Worcestershire sauce
¼ tsp. black pepper	1¼ C. water

Melt butter; add onion and brown sugar. Add other ingredients and simmer for 20 minutes. Paint rabbit with pastry brush. Cook at 325° for 1½ hours.

Aunt Helen's Rabbit

1 (2½ lb.) rabbit	1 egg
1 C. cornmeal	1 tsp. salt
2 tsp. baking powder	1¼ C. milk
1 C. sifted flour	Shortening for rabbit

Mix flour, baking powder, cornmeal, and salt. Add milk and egg. Mix until smooth. Dip rabbit and fry until brown.

Rabbit Casserole

3-4 lb. rabbit (cut in serving pieces)   1 tsp. salt
½ C. margarine (melted)   Pepper, to taste
2 eggs, slightly beaten with   ½ C. bread crumbs
  2 T. milk   2½ C. medium white sauce

Mix seasonings and bread crumbs. Dip rabbit into egg mixture then in crumbs. Brown lightly in margarine. Put in casserole dish and cover with white sauce. Bake, covered at 325° for 1½ hours. Serves 8.

Pressed Rabbit

3 C. broth   2 C. ground cooked meat
2 T. gelatin   Pepper, salt, onion salt (if desired)

Bring broth to boil; add gelatin that was soaked 5 minutes in small amount of cold water. Stir in meat and pour in loaf pan. Chill in refrigerator. Can add minced onion, pickle or celery.

Rabbit Sausage

Meat from baked or roasted rabbit, ½ lb. fresh side pork (sliced), pepper, salt sage, to taste. Grind coarse and fry. Make into patties.

Rabbit Casserole

In bottom of casserole, place small balls of rabbit sausage or ground rabbit meat. Add scant ⅓ C. rice — layer sliced carrots over rice, potatoes over carrots, onions over potatoes. Season with salt as you go. Pour 1 can tomato soup diluted with ½ C. water over casserole. Whole tomatoes can also be used instead of soup. Sprinkle cheese and paprika over top. Bake at 350° for 1½ hours. It's a whole meal in itself.

Rabbit 'N Dumplings

2 rabbits
1 or 2 bay leaves (optional)
½ tsp. garlic powder
(optional)

1 large or 2 small onions
(cut in large pieces)
Salt and pepper, to taste

Put rabbit in kettle, almost covered with water. Add seasonings and bring to a boil. Boil slowly until meat is tender, but doesn't fall off bone. Remove meat from broth and thicken with flour or cornstarch to consistency of gravy. Put rabbit in gravy, top with dumplings.

DUMPLINGS:
½ C. milk
2½ tsp. baking powder
¼ tsp. salt

1 to 1½ C. flour
1 medium egg

Mix all together and drop in broth.

Crock Rabbit

1-2 rabbits (cut-up)   *1 can cream of mushroom soup*

Place cut up rabbit into crock pot and set on "low" for 7 to 8 hours. Don't hurry this, it must be on "low". The taste is delicious despite the simplicity of the recipe. If you like tender without a lot of work, this will do it.

Little Critter Stew

3 rabbits or squirrels (cut-up)   *1 chopped onion*
3 qts. water   *2 cans drained tomatoes*
¼ C. diced bacon   *2 C. lima beans*
¼ tsp. pepper   *2 C. diced potatoes*
¼ tsp. cayenne   *2 C. corn*
2 tsp. salt

Place critters in large kettle with water and bring to boil. Simmer for 2 hours or until tender, skimming the surface occasionally. Remove meat from bones and return to water. Add bacon, pepper, cayenne, salt, onion, tomatoes, beans, and potatoes. Cook for 1 hour. Add corn and cook an additional for 10 minutes.

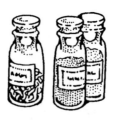

Rabbit with Prunes

Cut 1 rabbit and cover with water. Bring salted water to boil, cover, and simmer. Add 2 C. prunes and ½ C. raisins to rabbit, before it is tender. Cook until prunes and raisins are tender. Add 1 dozen crumbled ginger snap cookies.

Baked Raccoon

1 tender adult raccoon
4 large apples
2 medium onions (chopped)
3-4 T. butter

3-4 C. dry bread cubes
Sage, to taste
Salt
Pepper

Clean fresh coon and soak in strong salt water overnight or 1 whole day. When ready to prepare remove from water and dry thoroughly with towel. Fill cavity with mixture of seasoned bread, diced apples, and chopped onion. Butter outside meat and sprinkle with seasoning. Bake at 350° in open roaster for approximately 20 minutes per pound or until done. Discard filling and serve with applesauce.

Raccoon Sloppy Joes

1 raccoon
1 onion (chopped)
1 green pepper (chopped)
2 stalks celery (chopped)

1 can chopped mushrooms
1 C. barbecue sauce
1 tsp. Lawry's seasoning salt
Dash of pepper

Trim fat from raccoon, cut into large pieces. Pressure cook or boil in water until meat falls off bones. Drain and break meat up into heavy cooking pan. Add other ingredients and simmer approximately ½ hour, stirring occasionally. Add more barbecue sauce if needed. Serve on hamburger buns or homemade biscuits.

(97)

Coon Stew

4 lbs. raccoon (cut in cubes)   2-3 C. canned tomatoes
2-3 onions (sliced)   Carrots
Salt and pepper   Onions (cubed)
Bay leaf   Potatoes (cubed)
Dash of Worcestershire sauce   Turnips (cubed)

Brown meat slowly in Dutch oven. There should be enough fat within the tissues that no additional fat is required. Add onions during the last of the browning process so they won't scorch. Reduce heat; add enough tomatoes and liquid to cover the meat; season and cover. Simmer on low until almost tender, then add cubed vegetables of your choice. Continue to simmer until vegetables are tender. Season to your taste.

BBQ Raccoon

4½-5 lbs. dressed raccoon   ⅓ to ½ C. vinegar (cider)
1½ qts. cold water   ¼ tsp. black pepper
2½ T. salt   3-4 lbs. sweet potatoes
1 dry hot red pepper pod (4" long)

Preheat 400° oven. Dress raccoon. Leave no hair on meat. Remove scent glands, kernels under legs. Wrap in foil and chill thoroughly. When ready to cook, trim all but a thin layer of fat from raccoon, and remove all discolored spots. Wash well in lukewarm water. Place raccoon in 5 qt. pan. Add cold water, salt, and crushed pepper. Heat to boiling; cover. Reduce heat and simmer until almost tender, 1-1½ hours. Put raccoon in covered roaster. Drizzle vinegar inside and out. Sprinkle with black pepper and red pepper. Cover and bake for 30 minutes. Pare potatoes and boil for 15 minutes, uncovered. Drain and arrange around raccoon. Bake, uncovered until brown, about 45 minutes.

Coon and Dressing

Cut coon into small pieces and salt to taste. Cook in the inset pan of the pressure cooker for about an hour at 15 pounds pressure. Cook longer if it is an old and tough coon. When coon is tender, arrange pieces in a baking dish and cover with dressing made as follows:

Moisten 8 to 10 slices of dry bread with the juice cooked from the coon and add 2 eggs, 2 T. sage, ½ tsp. ground cloves, and 1 T. salt. Bake in 350° oven until the dressing is browned. This assures a tender, tasty coon without being too fat and greasy. Also good for possum.

BBQ Raccoon

4-5 lbs. raccoon (halved)
Water to cover
1½ T. salt
1 tsp. pepper

1 medium onion (chopped)
1 T. vinegar
18 oz. bottle BBQ sauce

In Dutch oven, precook raccoon in water for 1½ hours; drain well. Discard liquid and return meat to oven. Add seasoning and onion. Cover and cook over low heat, adding water to keep meat from sticking, 1 hour. Combine vinegar and BBQ sauce. Drain liquid from meat. Spoon sauce over meat and continue cooking 1-1½ hours or until meat is fork tender.

How to Cook Coon

Cut-up coon and boil in water with a little salt until tender. Place in shallow pan and sprinkle with a little sage; add 1 C. broth. Precook about 5 medium-size sweet potatoes, cut in half and place around coon. Bake in hot oven for 20 minutes.

Old Fashioned Coon

Put 1 coon in salt and soda water and let stand overnight. Take out of water next morning and wash 2 times and put in kettle and boil until tender. Put in a bread pan and put pepper and sage on it and bake. Serve with sweet potatoes.

Barbecued Raccoon

Raccoon   *Barbecue sauce*

Soak coon in salt water for several hours. Remove as much fat as possible. Cut-up coon and cover with water and cook until tender, changing water 2 to 3 times during cooking. Remove meat from bones and add favorite barbecue sauce and put in oven for about 1 hour. Serve on hamburger buns.

French Fried Rabbit

1 rabbit (cut in pieces)   ½ C. evaporated milk
Salt   2 eggs (beaten)
1 medium onion (sliced)   Cracker crumbs
2 T. flour

Parboil rabbit for 45 minutes in salted water in which onion has been added. Remove and drain on paper toweling. Mix flour, milk, and eggs. Dip rabbit in egg, then in crumbs. Fry in deep fat until golden.

Rabbit in Kettle

1 (2½ lb.) rabbit   2 qt. boiling water
  (cut in serving pieces)   2 C. diced potatoes
6 small white onions   ½ lb. fresh mushrooms (sliced)
1 bay leaf   ½ C. flour
1½ C. diced celery   ½ C. cold water
4½ tsp. salt   1 T. snipped parsley
1/8 tsp. pepper   Dash of Tabasco

Wash and dry cleaned rabbit. Place in kettle with onions, bay leaf, celery, salt, pepper, and water. Simmer, covered for 2 hours or until rabbit is nearly tender. Add potatoes, carrots, and mushrooms. Simmer, covered for 30 minutes or until all is tender. Blend flour with water. Stir into stew and cook until thickened. Add parsley and Tabasco sauce. Serves 6.

Rabbit

4 rabbits   1 tsp. salt
1 can mushroom soup   ½ tsp. pepper
3 C. water

In a small roaster put in all ingredients and let cook at 350° for about 1 hour.

Rabbit Sausage

6 lbs. rabbit meat
2 small onions
2 T. salt
2 tsp. pepper
¾ C. sweet milk

¼ tsp. paprika
1 bay leaf
½ tsp. sage
2 eggs
½ C. cracker crumbs

Mix well together and mold into patties and fry until browned. Can be cold packed in jars, filled with broth, and topped with 3 to 4 T. grease they were fried in. Process for 180 minutes.

Oven Fried Rabbit

1 rabbit (cleaned & cut-up)
Flour

Salt and pepper
Butter

Roll rabbit in flour. Melt a generous amount of butter in a large frying pan. Brown all sides of the rabbit pieces well. Remove the rabbit meat from the pan and put them ina baking pan with a cover. Pour melted butter over the pieces of meat. Salt and pepper. Add ½ C. of water. Bake in oven at 350° for about 1 hour. Serves family of 4.

Pan Fried Rabbit

Rabbits (cleaned)
1 egg (beaten)
1 T. water
Butter

Flour
Salt and pepper
Thyme

Cut young rabbits in serving pieces. Dip in mixture of egg and water. Roll in flour that has been seasoned with salt, pepper, and a pinch of thyme. Heat butter in heavy skillet. Brown rabbit over low heat until golden brown. Reduce heat until well done.

Fried Rabbit with Sour Cream Gravy

Rabbit (cut-up)
Salt
Black pepper
1 tsp. finely chopped garlic
4 T. butter

1 C. flour
4 T. oil
¼ C. chopped onions
1 C. chicken broth
1 C. sour cream

Sprinkle each piece with salt and pepper. Flour each piece thoroughly. Heat butter and oil in heavy skillet. Brown rabbit pieces. Cover and cook on lowest heat until tender. Remove meat to platter or dish. Pour off all but a thin flim of fat. Add chopped onion and garlic. Cook for 3 to 4 minutes. Pour in chicken stock. Boil briskly until stock is reduced by about a third. Turn down heat and with a whisk slowly beat in sour cream. Simmer only long enough to heat gravy through. Pour over rabbit or serve separately.

Fried Rabbit

2 rabbits (2-3 lbs. ea.)
2 egg yolks (beaten)
3 C. milk
1¼ C. flour

1 tsp. salt
½ C. Crisco
Parsley

Clean dressed rabbits and soak in cold salt water for 2 hours. Cut-up and dry off pieces. Combine egg yolks and 1 C. milk; add 1 C. flour a little at a time. Add salt and beat until smooth. Dip rabbit into batter and fry until brown, 15 to 20 minutes. Reduce heat and continue cooking until tender, 40 to 45 minutes, turning often. Make a gravy by adding remaining flour to the fat in pan. Add the remaining milk gradually, stirring constantly. Bring to boil. Salt and pepper and pour over fried rabbit. Garnish with chopped parsley. Serves 6.

Sweet-Sour Rabbit

2-3 lbs. tender young rabbit	1 C. pineapple chunks
¼ C. butter or oil	1 medium green pepper
1½ tsp. salt	(cut in thin half slices)
¼ tsp. pepper	1½ T. cornstarch
1 C. pineapple juice	¼ C. sugar
¼ C. vinegar	½ C. water

Heat fat in frying pan and brown rabbit over moderate heat. Season with salt and pepper. Add pineapple juice and vinegar. Cover pan and cook over low heat for 45 minutes or until tender. Add pineapple and green pepper, then cook a few minutes longer. Mix cornstarch and sugar; stir into the water. Stir this mixture gradually into liquid in the pan of rabbit and cook slowly for 5 minutes. Serve 4 to 6.

Fancy Rabbit

1 fryer rabbit (cut-up)	2 C. cream
½ lb. butter or margarine	1 C. beef or chicken bouillon
2 C. fresh sliced mushrooms	3 T. pimiento
1 C. rice	½ C. white wine
1 C. frozen peas	Salt and pepper, to taste

Saute' rabbit in the butter until golden brown; remove from pan. Saute' mushrooms in remaining butter or margarine. Add cream, bouillon, and wine to mushrooms, stirring constantly; set aside. Bring to boil 1 ¾ C. water and add ¾ tsp. salt; stir in 1 C. rice. Cover and cook over slow heat for approximately 30 minutes. Uncover pot for the last 5 minutes and continue to cook over slow heat, shaking the pot from time to time until grains are separated. Cook 1 C. frozen peas and add to rice; add 3 T. chopped pimientos.

To Serve: Place a mound of rice on plate and top with serving of rabbit. Spoon mushroom sauce over all and garnish with chopped parsley.

Hasenpfeffer

1 rabbit (cut in serving pieces)   2 tsp. salt
½ C. lemon juice   1 C. onions
1 C. butter   1 T. sugar
Bacon   ⅔ C. sour cream
¼ C. water   ¼ C. red wine (optional)
1 T. vinegar   Flour

Soak rabbit and cut in serving pieces overnight in enough cold water to cover, mixed with ½ C. lemon juice. Use part of butter to grease heavy roasting pan well. Put in the drained rabbit pieces and cut remainder of butter over top. Cover with strips of bacon. Add ¼ C. water, mixed with the vinegar and salt; sprinkle chopped onions over top and bake at 300° for about 2 hours or until tender and nicely browned. Shortly before it is done, caramelize the sugar and add to sauce in pan. Then add sour cream, mixed with the red wine (optional) and thicken the gravy with flour and water. Serve hot with small boiled potatoes. Serves 3 to 4.

Sweet and Sour Rabbit

1 fryer rabbit (3 lbs.)　　　½ tsp. cinnamon
Garlic powder, to taste　　　½ tsp. allspice
¼ tsp. black pepper　　　　1 medium onion
2 T. flour　　　　　　　　1½ C. water
2 T. oil or cooking fat

Mix flour, pepper, and garlic powder in paper bag and shake rabbit pieces in seasoned flour. Brown in Dutch oven or iron skillet. Sprinkle cinnamon and allspice on rabbit. Add onion and water; simmer or cook in a moderate oven (350°) for 2 to 3 hours or until tender. Remove onion and discard; remove rabbit and reserve cooking liquid. Remove meat from bones and dice meat. Place on a hot serving platter and spoon sauce over rabbit meat and serve with rice and garnish with fresh mint.

Beaver Stew

2 lbs. beaver meat　　　　1 onion (large)
2 stalks celery　　　　　　1 small pkg. frozen broccoli &
3 large carrots　　　　　　　cauliflower pieces
3 large potatoes　　　　　1 tsp. Lawry's seasoning salt
1 small rutabaga　　　　　¼ tsp. pepper
½ head cabbage　　　　　½ C. barley

Cut vegetables into small bite-size pieces. Cut beaver into bite-size pieces and put into 4-quart pot. Add water and seasonings; boil until meat is tender (approximately ½ hour). Add vegetables and ½ C. barley. Simmer for approximately 1 hour or until all vegetables are tender.

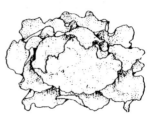

Beaver Tail Roast

1 Beaver tail
1 C. red wine
1 C. water
1 large onion (chopped)
Cracker crumbs
Lemon juice

½ C. vinegar
1 tsp. salt
Flour
Egg
3 T. melted butter

Marinate tail for 24 hours in wine, water, and onion. Dry tail and scrape carefully. Parboil until tender in enough water to cover. To the water add ½ C. vinegar and 1 tsp. salt. Dry tail again. Dust with flour and dip into beaten eggs, then cracker crumbs. Pour 3 T. melted butter over tail. Roast on rack in a 350° oven until brown and tender. Serve with hot lemon juice. Serves 2.

Raccoon

Raccoon meat is very dark. Remove all fat from raccoon outside and inside, as well as fat imbedded between the strong bands of muscle. Remove all fat. Most important is to remove the scent glands found under the forelegs and along the spine in the small of the back. These glands are usually pea-shape and are waxy texture; reddish to yellow in color. Never cut these glands or let them come in contact with the meat.

Roast Coon 'N Dressing

1 coon	1 large apple (diced)
1 pkg. single loaf frozen	1½ tsp. sage
bread dough	Salt and pepper, to taste
1 medium onion (chopped)	

Take coon that has been cleaned, scent glands removed and soak in soda water for 2 hours. Solution: 2 T. vinegar and water to cover; rinse coon and dry. Place coon in roaster, covered with 1½ C. water in bottom of roaster. Roast at 350° until tender. Add dressing about 45 minutes before coon is done. After dressing has been added, roast 20 minutes, uncovered to brown coon.

STUFFING: Let frozen bread rise in its package. Make into biscuits and let rise again. Bake biscuits at 325° for 15 minutes. When cool, put in 2 C. of cold water that the sage, salt, and pepper has been added (enough water to moisten all biscuits). Break apart and stuff biscuits with onions and apples. Arrange biscuits around coon in drippings. Pour 1 qt. tomatoes over coon and stuffing and finish baking, uncovered. Garnish with chopped parsley.

Preparations of Smoking Game or Fowl

When preparing your game or fowl for smoking, make wooden pegs; ¾-inch around and 2-inches long to hold open the cavities of the game or fowl while smoking. This will let the heat and smoke penetrate all sides. For larger bird, use longer pegs; small fish, etc., the shorter pegs.

Roast Raccoon with Veggies

Clean and remove scent glands from coon as directed. Soak coon and rinse and dry. Score meat and press slices of onion into splits. Roll coon pieces, best cut in serving pieces or whole in flour that the following has been added:

1 C. flour	½ tsp. curry powder
1 tsp. salt	¼ tsp. pepper
1½ tsp. paprika	Vegetables as shown below

Brown raccoon in oil. Put in roasting pan; with drippings that 1½ C. water has been added. Grind 1 green pepper and 2 carrots; spread this on raccoon. Bake at 350° for 45 minutes, covered. Meanwhile, prepare 6 medium white potatoes, 3 small sweet potatoes, 6 carrots, 3 stalks celery (cubed), 3 apples (peeled and halved), onions may be added. Arrange around coon and bake an additional 30 minutes, covered and cook until tender. Serves 6 to 8.

Fricasseed Raccoon

1 raccoon	1½ tsp. salt
¾ C. flour	¼ tsp. black pepper
1 tsp. paprika	3 T. oil or bacon drippings

Clean raccoon as directed and soak in solution of soda and water; rinse and dry. Cut in serving pieces. Dredge raccoon pieces in flour that has paprika, salt, and pepper added. Brown in oil. Place in roaster. Add 2 C. water; cover and simmer until tender. For variety, add 2 onions (sliced thin), added to the last 30 minutes or roasting, gives a delicious flavor. Variety II: Add sliced sweet potatoes to the last 30 minutes of roasting, gives raccoon a tang. Sprinkle with juice of 1 lemon the last 10 minutes of roasting or until sweet potatoes are tender.

Roast Raccoon and Sweet Potatoes

1 raccoon
2 onions (whole)
2 apples (whole)
6 medium sweet potatoes
6 slices bacon

3 stalks celery
Salt and pepper, to taste
2 C. water that 2 beef cube of
    bouillon has been added

Clean raccoon as directed. Soak in solution of 2 T. water to cover raccoon; soak for 2 hours and rinse and dry. Place raccoon in roasting pan with 2 C. water, onion, apples, and celery into cavity. Roast in covered roaster for 1 hour at 350°. Meanwhile, peel sweet potatoes and wrap the bacon and fasten with toothpicks. Uncover roaster and arrange sweet potatoes around raccoon. Baste raccoon every 30 minutes of roasting time; add more water if needed. Roast until raccoon is tender and also the sweet potatoes. Remove raccoon from roasting pan; take onion, apple, and celery out and discard. Arrange sweet potatoes around raccoon. Gravy may be made from juices in roaster. Garnish with apple rings and parsley.

Roast Beaver

A beaver has scent glands located between the forelegs, under the thighs, and along the spine. These should be carefully removed immediately after the animal has been skinned, but be sure not to cut into them. Remove all surface fat and cover meat with a solution of 1 tsp. soda to 1 qt. water. Simmer for 10 minutes. Put meat in roaster, cover with sliced onions, strips of bacon, salt, and roast in moderate oven (350°). Beaver should be cooked until meat falls off the bones.

Beaver Patties

1 beaver (ground)	½ tsp. salt
1 onion (chopped)	Black pepper, to taste
½ tsp. celery salt	¼ C. milk
3 T. margarine	¼ C. bread crumbs

Mix all ingredients together, except the margarine. Melt margarine in fry pan; form patties and fry in hot oil as you would a hamburger. Fry until well done. For added flavor, pour a can of your favorite soup over the beaver burgers and simmer for 20 minutes.

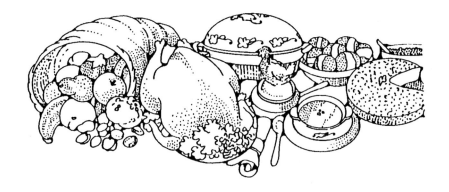

Notes

BIG CRITTERS THAT STOMP AROUND IN THE WOODS

Index

All About Large Game

Hunters are urged to handle their animals promptly. Immediate care of the animal helps to insure higher quality meat.

Once the animal has been killed, the first thing to do is bleed it. The more blood that is drained, the better the meat will be. Blood that remains lowers the quality of the meat. Dress the animal carefully. Remove scent glands and wipe body cavity well. Use a dry cloth or dry leaves for this; wet meat spoils quickly.

Cool quickly. Experienced hunters recommend hanging the dressed deer in a shaded spot with good air circulation. Prop flanks open with an 8-inch or 10-inch stick.

Disagreeable flavor is usually traced to: (1) inadequate bleeding; (2) delay or carelessness in field dressing, and (3) failure to cool deer at once.

Cool transporation, too, is important. Keep the carcass as cool as possible on the trip home. Use car top or back of station wagon. Never the hot car radiator.

The ideal situation when hunting a long way from home is to find a meat processor who can cut up your animal, quick freeze it and supply you with dry ice to get your meat home.

To improve flavor, age carcass for several days in refrigerator or cold area. Leave skin on during aging to prevent meat from dehydrating and turning dark.

All fat should be trimmed to reduce the strong flavor.

Quick Venison Chili

1 qt. canned venison
1 qt. canned tomatoes
1 large can chili style beans

2 T. chili powder
Pepper
1 diced onion

Mix ingredients together; heat and serve. Great for hunting trips around campfire.

Chili

4 T. butter or drippings
1 lb. game 'burger'
2 sliced onions
Chili powder, to taste

1 shredded green pepper
   (if desired)
2 (15 oz. ea.) cans Mexican
   beans in chili gravy

Brown meat and onions in fat (start with frozen meat, if necessary), breaking the meat in small pieces as it browns; drain. Add green pepper and chili beans. Cover and simmer for 10 minutes. Check seasoning and add more chili powder, if desired and simmer for 10 minutes more.

Venison Patties in Milk Gravy

1½ lbs. ground venison
½ lb. ground pork
1 T. poultry seasoning
1/8 tsp. ground nutmeg
Salt and pepper, to taste

3 T. fat, reserved from browning
3 T. flour
1½ C. cold water
1½ C. cold milk

Mix well together the venison, pork, and seasonings; form into patties. Flour outside and brown well in fat; remove to plate. To reserved fat, add flour and mix well, scraping bottom of skillet. Slowly add water and milk, stirring with wire whisk or fork. Bring slowly to boil and stir until it thickens. Salt and pepper, to taste. Place patties in gravy, turn heat down and simmer, covered for 25 minutes. Serve with mashed potatoes.

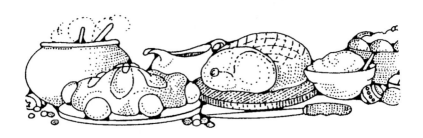

Venison Short Ribs

3 lbs. venison short ribs
1 T. salt
1 qt. water
1 tsp. paprika
1 large onion (chopped)

½ C. catsup
¼ C. vinegar
2 T. water
2 tsp. chili powder
3 T. bacon drippings

Soak venison ribs in salt water solution for several hours or overnight. Wash the ribs after soaking and parboil for about 30 minutes in pressure cooker at 10 pounds pressure. Remove from pressure cooker and place in frying pan. Mix the last 7 ingredients together and pour over ribs. Bake at 375° for about 1 hour or until meat is tender and browned. Serves 4 to 6.

Deer Jerky

1 T. salt
¼ tsp. pepper
3 drops of Tabasco sauce
½ T. garlic salt

¼ T. Worcestershire sauce
Dash of oregano or thyme
1 lb. raw venison
Water

Cut venison into ¼-inch strips. Combine remaining ingredients and pour over meat, adding water, if needed to cover meat. Refrigerate overnight in mixture. Drain meat and pat dry. Bake at 120°-150° for 4 hours.

Venison Tidbits

Bacon
Venison
2 C. water

Salt
Black pepper
½ C. Worcestershire sauce

Cut pieces of venison into 1-inch squares. Take a thin slice of bacon and cut it just long enough to wrap around the meat. Secure with a toothpick. Make about 2 dozen. Put in a cast-iron skillet. Add 2 C. water, salt, lots of black pepper, and ½ C. Worcestershire sauce. Boil rapidly until water is nearly gone. Reduce heat and cover skillet; continue cooking at lower temperature until meat is brown. The meat will be very rich.

Crock Pot Deer Roast

1 deer roast (for chuck roast
  or rump roast) (completely defat)
3 C. water

½ C. chopped onion
1 tsp. basil
Salt and pepper

Brown roast well on both sides in bacon grease or lard. Put in crock pot. Add remaining ingredients. Cook all day or till well done.

Deer Summer Sausage

4 lbs. deer burger
1 tsp. peppercorn (cracked)
1 tsp. onion salt
1 tsp. garlic salt

1 tsp. liquid smoke
1 tsp. mustard seed (chopped)
4 T. Morton Tender Quick salt
2 T. brown sugar

Mix together and make into 6 rolls. Wrap in foil and store in refrigerator for 24 hours. Bake at 350° for 1 hour. Let stand in grease until cool, turning several times.

Deer Roast

Deer roast
1 pkg. onion soup mix

1 can mushroom or celery soup

Cut all fat from roast. Put roast in foil. Pour soup and soup mix over roast. Seal foil and put in pan with lid. Bake at 275°-300° for 4 to 5 hours.

Yogurt Marinade for Venison

1 small container plain yogurt   *2 T. Lawry's seasoned salt*
1 large onion (diced)   *2-3 lbs. venison steaks or chops*

Combine all but meat in bowl. Pour into strong plastic bag. Add venison and seal bag. Squeeze to distribute marinade over meat. Refrigerate for 3 to 4 hours or overnight, turning bag occasionally. Grill or broil meat to your taste.

Venison and Rice

1½ lbs. venison   *1 can cream of mushroom soup*
1½ T. vegetable oil   *½ C. dry sherry*
2 large onions (cut in rings)   *1½ tsp. garlic salt*
4 ozs. sliced mushrooms   *3 C. hot cooked rice*

Cut venison in thin strips. Brown meat in oil. Add onions and saute' until tender-crisp. Blend all but rice. Pour over venison. Reduce heat and simmer for 1 hour or until tender or cover and bake at 350° until tender. Serve over rice.

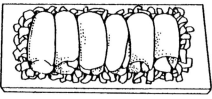

Deer Jerky Recipe

1 T. salt   *¼ T. Worcestershire sauce*
¼ tsp. pepper   *Dash of oregano or thyme*
3 drops of Tabasco sauce   *1 lb. raw venison*
½ T. garlic salt   *Water*

Cut venison into ¼-inch strips. Combine remaining ingredients and pour over meat, adding water, if needed to cover meat. Refrigerate overnight in mixture. Drain meat and pat dry. Bake at 120°-150° for 4 hours.

Sweet and Sour Meat Balls

1 medium onion
1 qt. Cookie's BBQ sauce
1 tsp. salt

2 lbs. ground venison
1 C. any flavor jelly
½ tsp. pepper

Dice onion and mix with venison. Add salt and pepper; mix well. Make meatballs and brown them in hot oil. Remove meatballs and place on paper towel to remove excess oil. In a 2-quart pan mix BBQ sauce and jelly. Heat until bubbly and jelly is well dissolved. Place meatballs in a baking dish. Pour BBQ mixture over meatballs. Bake at 300° for 40 minutes. (Note: This is a good crock pot dish. Any old or sugared jelly works great.)

More Meatballs

½ lb. ground venison
¼ C. cracker crumbs
1 T. catsup
1 tsp. horseradish

1 tsp. mustard
½ tsp. onion powder
½ tsp. salt

Mix all ingredients and form into small balls. Bake at 350° until browned and cooked through. Serve alone or mixed with your favorite sauce.

Still More Venison Meatballs

2 lbs. ground venison or beef
1 beaten egg
1 large grated onion
1 (12 oz.) bottle chili sauce

1 (10 oz.) bottle grape jelly
Juice of 1 lemon
Salt, to taste

Combine meat, egg, and onion. Make this mixture into small balls. In a large saucepan, combine remaining ingredients and bring to a boil. Drop the meatballs into boiling sauce and cook until done (10 to 15 minutes). Serve in chafing dish or crock pot to keep warm. These may be frozen and heated up when needed.

Party Meatballs

1 lb. ground venison
¼ tsp. oregano
½ tsp. garlic salt
1 jar favorite barbecue sauce

*Salt, pepper, and onion salt
(to taste)
3 small squares crackers
(in fine crumbs)*

Mix all ingredients and form into meatballs. Bake for 15 to 20 minutes; remove from oven. Drain grease and cover with barbecue sauce. Keep warm while serving.

Venison Chili Dip

2 lbs. ground venison
2 lbs. Velveeta cheese
½ C. sliced jalapeno (or to taste)

*2 cans Hormel Chili
without beans*

Brown venison and drain. Cube Velveeta cheese. Place all ingredients in crock pot on high heat, stirring occasionally. Turn to low heat when cheese is melted. Serve warm with tortilla chips.

Canned Deer, Moose, Elk, Etc.

1 animal

Cube pieces of meat. Pack raw meat tightly in jars. Put lids on. Pressure cook for 90 minutes at 10 lbs. for quarts; 75 minutes at 10 lbs. for pints. Great for round steaks, just drop them in wide mouth quart jars. To use pour out in skillet and reheat with your choice of mushrooms, mushroom soup, onions or your favorite Swiss steak recipe. Quick and easy! Cubed meat is great in chili, casserole dishes, over noodles or biscuits, in stews and soups, etc.

Mountain Sheep Roast

Roast from hind leg or saddle   *Garlic or rosemary*
Lemon juice   *Salt and pepper*
Cookin oil

Remove all fat possible, rub with lemon juice, and brush with cooking oil. Season with salt and pepper. Insert slivers of garlic in the roast or sprinkle a few leaves of rosemary in the bottom of the roaster. Sear in preheated (475°) oven until browned, about 20 minutes. Add water to cover bottom of pan and roast at 300° (25 minutes per pound) until tender, basting frequently.

Canned Deer

Deer meat　　　　　　　　　*Salt*
Beef bouillon cubes　　　　　*Beef suet*

Cut meat small enough to fit in quart or pint jars. Fill jars 4/5 full of deer meat. For quarts, add 2 beef bouillon cubes and 1 tsp. salt; add beef suet to remaining space in jar leaving ½-inch air space. Place rings and flats on jars and put in pressure canner at 10 lbs. for 90 minutes (quarts); 70 minuts (pints). Great for stews and sandwiches!

Tomato Eggplant Vension Casserole

1 qt. canned deer　　　　　　*1 medium eggplant*
2 T. oil　　　　　　　　　　*1 C. sharp cheese (grated)*
½ tsp. oregano　　　　　　　*½ C. chopped onion*
1 T. flour　　　　　　　　　*2 large tomatoes (sliced)*

Peel and cube eggplant. Boil in salt water until tender, not soft. Drain and set aside. Put canned deer in casserole dish and cover with tomato slices. Add eggplant and season with oregano and top with cheese. Bake at 350° for 30 to 40 minutes.

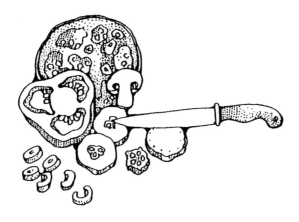

Deer Zucchini Casserole

1 qt. canned deer or
  1 lb. ground beef (browned)
1 small zucchini (sliced)
1 C. Cheddar cheese

1 onion (chopped)
1 can tomatoes
¾ C. instant rice
¼ C. margarine

Saute' zucchini and onion in margarine. Add tomatoes. In a 1-quart casserole dish add ½ of zucchini-tomato mixture, then rice, then can of deer, and other ½ of zucchini-tomato mixture. Bake at 350° for 30 minutes, covered. Uncover and add cheese. Bake 10 minutes longer.

Deer and Biscuits

1 qt. canned deer
3 C. self-rising flour
2 T. cornstarch

6 T. cooking oil
1 C. milk

Heat canned deer in skillet. Salt and pepper to taste (add fresh morsels if you find any). Mix cornstarch with water and add to meat to thicken. Mix flour, oil, and milk. Pat or roll on floured surface. Cut out and place on greased baking sheet. Bake at 400° approximately 10 minutes. To make sourdough biscuits, add 1 C. sourdough starter to mix.

Hot Venison Sandwich

1 jar of canned deer

Gravy mix packet

Remove beef suet from canned deer. Warm meat. Prepare gravy meat according to directions. Prepare mashed potatoes, put meat and gravy on top.

Venison Stew

1 jar canned deer
2 medium-size cans mixed
  vegetables
2 medium potatoes (cut-up small)

2 stalks celery (cut-up)
½ C. water
3 bay leaves

Combine ingredients in crock pot. Cook on Low for 6 to 8 hours or High for 3 to 6 hours. Remove bay leaves before eating. If any leftovers, put in container and freeze for a meal another day.

Barbecue Venison Sandwiches

1 jar canned deer

Barbecue sauce

Remove beef suet from canned deer. Add barbecue sauce and warm through. Serve on buns.

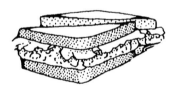

Two Hour Jerky

Any amount of meat (up to 10 lbs.,
  cut into ¼-inch strips)
2 qts. water

½ pt. vinegar
2 C. salt
2 T. black pepper

Add all ingredients and boil for 5 minutes. Roll any excess moisture from meat with a rolling pin or by hand. Place on oven racks and cook for 1½ to 2 hours at 200° with door open (cracked) on oven. Remove meat and paint with basting brush using A-1 sauce or open pit sauce or horseradish and ketchup mixture or other seasoned sauces.

Deer Jerky

½ C. Worcestershire sauce
¼ C. soy sauce
1/8 tsp. (about) pepper

½ T. garlic & salt, to taste
2-4 lbs. lean cuts of venison

Slice meat as thin as possible with the grain. Marinate overnight in sauce. Dry in oven at 140°-160° for 4 to 6 hours. Store in airtight containers. Can take a little longer to dry if cut thick. Be sure to remove all the fat from the meat before drying.

Venison Jerky

4-6 lbs. (approx.) lean cuts
   of venison
Liquid smoke
8-10 drops Tobasco sauce

1-1½ C. salt
1 C. sugar
1 gallon water

Trim off all fat and cut meat with the grain ½-inch thick by 2-4 inches wide by 4-8 inches long. Cover with brine for 8 to 12 hours. Drain and dry at room temperature. Season additionally to taste with black pepper, Lawry's seasoned salt, etc. Let your conscience be your guide. Dry in oven at around 200° or as low as possible - try not to cook. meat will dry best with oven cracked open and meat placed directly on oven racks or on cake cooling racks.

For Brine: Dissolve salt and sugar into 1 gallon tepid water. Add approximately 1 T. liquid smoke. Adjust ingredients to suit individual taste. (Note: Tougher cuts of venison make chewier jerky. It is best to remove major sinews though. You can dry to varying degrees from very flexible to cracker dry. Keep refrigerated if storing for a length of time, although the jerky will not spoil, it can get rancid or moldy.)

Mexican Deer

1 pt. canned venison
¼ C. chopped onion
4 eggs
1 (8 oz.) can tomato sauce
1 (5⅓ oz.) can evaporated milk

1 (1½ oz.) env. enchilada
   sauce mix
⅓ C. sliced pitted ripe olives
2 C. tortilla corn chips
1 C. shredded Cheddar cheese

In skillet cook meat and onion until onions are tender. Drain and spread meat mixture in a 10x6x2-inch baking dish. Beat together eggs, tomato sauce, evaporated milk, and enchilada sauce mix; pour over meat. Sprinkle with olive slices and top with chips. Bake, uncovered at 350° until center is set, 20 to 25 minutes. Sprinkle with cheese and bake until cheese melts, 3 to 5 minutes. Makes 6 servings. (Can substitute ground venison for canned and cook until brown with onions.)

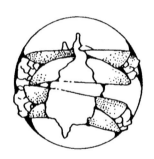

More Venison Jerky

1½ lbs. flank steak
1 tsp. seasoned salt
1 T. liquid smoke
1 tsp. Tender Quick salt
¼ C. soy sauce

⅓ tsp. garlic salt or powder
⅓ tsp. black pepper
1 tsp. Accent
1 tsp. onion powder or salt
¼ C. Worcestershire sauce

Trim off all fat from meat. Cut meat into 1/8-inch to ¼-inch thick pieces (cuts better if partially frozen). Combine seasoning and sauces. Put meat ina a 9x9x2-inch glass pan and cover with seasoning and sauce mixture. Let set overnight. Dry in oven at 140° for 6 to 8 hours. (NOTE: Meat should be in a single layer.) Makes about ½ lb.

Venison Salami

4 lbs. ground venison	2½ tsp. mustard seed
1 lb. ground pork	2½ tsp. coarse ground pepper
5 tsp. Morton Tender Quick curing	1 tsp. liquid smoke
salt (well rounded)	

Mix all ingredients well and let stand in refrigerator for 2 days. Remove and mix well and refrigerate for 2 more days. On 5th day make into sausage rolls and place on cookie sheet in preheated oven (140°). Turn every hour for 8 hours. (NOTE: Salami should be approximately 2½-inches from top of oven. You can substitute 3 lbs. ground venison and 2 lbs. ground beef or use 5 lbs. ground beef instead.)

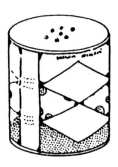

Summer Sausage

5 lbs. lean ground venison (cut-up)	2½ tsp. mustard seed
5 tsp. (rounded) Morton Tender	2½ tsp. cracked black pepper
Quick salt	2½ tsp. garlic salt

Mix items above well (if you don't have a well, mix above anything - such as a table, the floor, etc.). Cover and refrigerate, removing to knead well once each day for the next 3 days. On the 5th day, form the meat into 4 rolls. Lay on broiler pan or cookie sheet and bake at 140° for 8 to 10 hours, turning every 2 hours. Cool and eat.

1st day - make sausage	4th day - knead
2nd day - knead	5th day - bake
3rd day - knead	

Pickled Deer Heart

PICKLING SOLUTION:
3 C. white vinegar   *3 tsp. (heaping) pickling spice*
1 C. water   *¾ C. white sugar*

Simmer for 30 minutes. Remove fat from heart and boil for 2 hours. Put in pickling solution and refrigerate. Can be eaten in 24 hours.

"Okra" Chili (Jalapeno)

3 lbs. ground venison   *½ can tomato soup*
1 medium onion   *Salt and pepper, to taste*
3 medium cans kidney beans   *1 C. jalapeno peppers (sliced)*
1 jar Pace picante sauce (hot)

Brown meat, onion, salt, pepper, and hot peppers. Add remaining ingredients and simmer for ½ hour.

Chili of Venison

1 lb. ground venison   *Tomato juice*
4 C. diced potatoes   *Chili powder*
1 can chili beans   *Onion, to taste*
1 can stewed tomatoes

Boil potatoes until almost done. Brown ground venison and onions, if desired. Pour chili beans and tomatoes into large pan; add browned venison and boiled potatoes. Season, to taste and then add tomato juice to desired consistency. Simmer for at least ½ hour.

Venison Stew

2 lbs. venison
4 potatoes
2 onions
4 carrots
4 sticks celery
1 green pepper

1 pkg. beef gravy mix
Juice from canned venison
  (if available)
Salt and pepper
Seasoning salt
Water

Trim venison of any fat. Cut venison and potatoes into ¾-inch cubes. Slice carrots, celery, and onions into bite-size pieces. Combine these ingredients in a Dutch oven or large heavy kettle. Add just from any canned venison, gravy mix, salt, pepper, and season to taste, then fill with water so all ingredients are covered. Cover kettle and boil until vegetables are tender, stirring occasionally. Serves about 6 hearty appetites. The amount of ingredients can vary according to taste or number of people.

Sweet and Sour Stew - Venison

1½ lbs. venison steak
  (1-inch cubes)
1½ T. cooking oil
1 (12 oz.) can beer
2 beef bouillon cubes
1 T. horseradish
2 tsp. steak sauce (A-1)
1 medium onion (sliced)

3 drops Tabasco sauce
1 tsp. thyme
½ tsp. dill weed
¼ tsp. allspice
¼ tsp. salt
Dash of pepper
Parsley or watercress for garnish

Brown the venison cubes in the oil in a heavy skillet. Add the rest of the ingredients and the seasonings (except the garnish). Simmer for 2½ hours with a lid on skillet. Add water during simmering, if necessary. Thicken the stew with cornstarch (2 T. dissolved in a couple ounces of cold water). Serve over a bed of cooked, buttered noodles. Garnish with parsley or watercress. Serves 4.

Oven Venison Stew

2 C. potatoes (diced)
2 C. carrots (sliced)
2 C. celery (diced)
1 large onion (diced)
Salt and pepper, to taste

1½ lbs. venison
   (cut into bite-size pieces)
1 large or 2 small cans
   tomato soup

Mix all ingredients together in large baking dish with a lid. Bake, covered at 275° for 5 hours. Do not uncover or stir.

Venison Stew

2 lbs. lean venison (1-inch cubes)
3 T. cooking oil
1 medium onion (cut small)
3 stalks celery (cut ¾-inch pieces)
2 cloves garlic (diced)
4 T. flour
1 (16 oz.) can tomatoes (chopped)
6-10 drops Tabasco sauce

1 (10 oz.) can tomato juice or V-8
1 (12 oz.) can beer
½ tsp. thyme
2 tsp. Worcestershire sauce
3 carrots (cut in ½-inch chunks)
2 C. potatoes (cut ½-inch)
1 C. beef stock or bouillon
   stock brought to a boil

Brown venison in oil in heavy pot. Remove meat and add onions, celery, and garlic to remaining oil and juices; cook until tender. Do not brown. Add flour and stir in well. Add boiling stock, stirring until smooth. Add tomatoes, juices, beer, spices, and venison; stir until mixed. Reduce heat and simmer for 1 hour. Add carrots and simmer for 1 hour more, covered. Add potatoes and cook until tender, about 45 minutes. Serves 6 to 8.

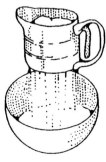

Oven Stew

2 lbs. lean stew meat of venison,
elk, moose or beef
1 large onion (thinly sliced &
separated into rings)
6 carrots (about, sliced into
½-inch chunks)
1 rib celery (sliced into ½-inch chunks)

3 potatoes (peeled & cut into
½-inch chunks)
2 tsp. sugar
2 tsp. salt
2 tsp. tapioca
1 C. tomato juice

Place meat in bottom of 4-quart casserole dish. Cover meat with vegetables. Mix sugar, salt, and tapioca. Sprinkle over vegetables. Add tomato juice and cover tightly. Bake at 250° for 5 hours. Do Not Peek!

More Venison Stew

1 lb. venison (cut in chunks)
2 C. water
½ tsp. lemon juice
½ tsp. Worcestershire sauce
½ clove garlic (minced)
½ medium onion (sliced)
1 small bay leaf (crumbled)

1 tsp. salt
1/8 tsp. pepper
Pinch of allspice
½ tsp. sugar
3 carrots
(cut into bite-size pieces)
2 potatoes (diced)

Stir all ingredients together in a covered baking dish. Cover tightly and bake at 325° for 2 hours.

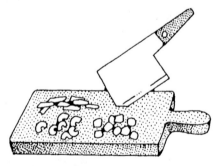

Loin Cubes of Deer

When you are butchering your deer or when you have it butchered, save the end of the loin and cut it up in about 2-inch cubes.

1 lb. 2-inch cubed deer loin   *1 large onion (cut in 1/8's)*
2 medium green peppers (quartered)   *Italian salad dressing*
16 morel mushrooms (whole) or   *Salt and pepper*
     16 large button mushrooms

Kabob all ingredients and cook over medium heat on grill turning twice, cook for 25 minutes, covering with Italian dressing each time you turn. Serves 4. Serve with burgundy wine.

Venison Kabobs

1-2 lbs. venison steak (cubed)   *Greenpeppers (sliced)*
Bottled French dressing   *Water chestnuts*
Mushrooms   *Small onions*
Pineapple chunks

Place cubed venison in a bowl. Pour enough French dressing over meat to coat well. Marinate for 1 hour or more. Skewer meat, mushrooms, pineapple, peppers, water chestnuts, and onions on skewers according to individual taste. Grill over charcoal, basting lightly with dressing.

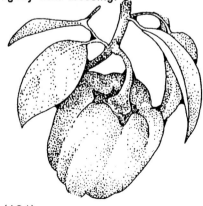

(131)

Cabbage Roll Casserole of Venison

2 lbs. venison (ground)
1 small head cabbage
1 pkg. beef Rice-A-Roni
1 can stewed tomatoes

1 medium onion
Mozzarella cheese, to taste
(we like a pound)

Brown meat and cook with cabbage and onion until vegetables are almost done. Add salt and pepper, to taste; let set. Cook Rice-A-Roni according to package directions, replacing some of the water with stewed tomatoes. Now layer meat mixture with rice and cheese in baking dish until all used up. Then just bake until heated through. (Can be refrigerated or frozen and baked at another time.)

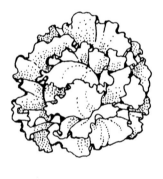 

Venison Pie

1 lb. ground venison
1 C. water
½ C. finely chopped onion
½ C. fine dry bread crumbs

1 tsp. salt
Dash ground sage
Dash ground nutmeg
Pastry for a 2-crust 9-inch pie

Brown the meat in skillet; drain off any excess fat. Add water, onion, crumbs, and seasonings. Simmer, covered for 5 minutes, stirring occasionally. Line a 9-inch pie plate with pastry. Turn meat mixture into crust. Adjust top crust and seal edges. Cut slits in top for escape of steam. Bake at 400° until crust is golden brown, approximately 35 to 40 minutes.

(132)

Venison-Stuffed Acorn Squash

1 medium acorn squash
1 pt. canned venison or
  ½ lb. ground venison
2 T. chopped onion
2 T. chopped celery
2 T. all-purpose flour

¼ tsp. salt
¼ tsp. ground sage
¾ C. milk
½ C. cooked rice
¼ C. shredded sharp cheese
Pepper

Cut squash in half and discard seeds. Sprinkle squash with a little salt. Bake, cut side down in small baking dish at 350° until tender, 45 to 50 minutes. Cook meat, onion, and celery until onions are clear; drain. Stir in flour, salt, and sage. Add milk. Cook and stir until thickened and bubbly. Stir in rice. Turn squash side up in dish; fill and bake, uncovered at 350° for 30 minutes. Sprinkle with pepper and top with cheese. Bake until cheese melts, about 3 minutes. Serves 2.

Venison Casserole

1 lb. ground venison (browned)
1 C. diced celery
1 medium onion (chopped)
1 can cream of chicken soup
1 can cream of mushroom soup

2 C. warm water
½ C. uncooked rice
¼ C. soy sauce
Salt, to taste
Pepper, to taste

Mix all ingredients and pour into baking dish with a cover. Bake, covered for 30 minutes. Sprinkle a can of Chinese noodles over top and bake for 15 minutes longer.

Big Game Wild Rice Casserole

1 lb. hamburger (deer, elk, etc.)
¼ C. wild rice (uncooked)
¼ C. white rice (uncooked)
1 can cream of mushroom soup

1 can chicken with rice soup
2 C. chopped celery
3-4 dashes soy sauce

Mix all together and bake at 350° for 2 hours, covered. Stir occasionally and add milk if too dry.

Venison Nacho Casserole

1 T. vegetable oil
1 C. chopped onion
1 tsp. minced garlic
1½ lbs. ground deer meat
1 (15 oz.) can tomato sauce
1 packet taco seasoning mix
1 (20 oz.) can red kidney beans

2 C. (8 oz.) shredded Cheddar
  cheese (divided)
1 (8 oz.) bag taco chips
½ C. taco sauce
½ C. chopped scallions (optional)
Sour cream (optional)
Avocado slices (optional)

In a large skillet heat oil over medium-high heat. Add onion and garlic. Saute' for 3 minutes; add deer burger, breaking it up while frying. Cook until brown, stirring often. Drain off any excess grease. Stir in tomato sauce and taco seasoning mix. Remove from heat and set aside. Rinse and drain kidney beans in strainer. Toss with 1 C. of the shredded Cheddar cheese. Reserve remaining cheese for sprinkling on top of casserole. Grease a shallow 2-quart casserole dish (can use a non-stick cooking spray). Line bottom of dish with ⅓ of the taco chips. Layer cheese-bean mixture. Cover bean mixture with ⅓ of the taco chips, then spoon meat mixture over this layer of chips. Then top with last ⅓ of chips arranging them neatly over meat mixture. Now drizzle taco sauce over chips and sprinkle with remaining cheese and scallions. Bake at 375° for 25 minutes until cheese is melted. Serve with sour cream and avocado slices, if desired. Serves 6.

Venison

A hunter is judged by the condition of the carcass he brings in. All fur bearing animals should be eviscerated at once and skinned as soon as possible. The gamey glands should be removed. There are four sets of these glands or "kernels" on the legs; two are found under the forelegs and two in each thigh. They are brownish, yellow, or red in color and oval or round in shape. Glands may be found along the small of the back. In skinning the animal, be careful not to let fur touch flesh, wiping or washing. All shot and blood clots should be removed promptly. The carcass should be chilled for at least 2 or 3 days. At this time wipe the carcass out with a solution of 1 lemon (juice only) to a quart of water. The best rule is to treat deer, antelope, and elk as you would domestic animals. After shooting the animal, clean the carcass as soon as possible, and cool carcass promptly to obtain the fullest flavor. Then it should be cut and stored properly or cooked according to the individual recipe.

Uncle Fred's Broiled Venison Steak

2 lbs. venison steak
(1-inch thick, which has
been marinated)

Salt and pepper, to taste
1 clove garlic

Rub steak with garlic. Place on broiler pan and broil for 12 minutes. Then turn and brush with butter. Broil for 12 more minutes. Salt and pepper; serve hot. Note: Always serve venison very hot.

MARINADE FOR STEAK: ⅓ C. lemon juice, ⅔ C. oil, 2 cloves garlic (minced fine). Marinate steak for 8 to 10 hours in covered dish in refrigerator. Drain well before broiling. Serves 4 to 5.

NOTE: This marinade may be used to marinate venison roast or chops.

Mighty Good Venison Swiss Steak

2 lbs. venison steak
3 large onions (sliced)
3 medium stalks celery
  (cut in 1-inch cubes)
1 clove garlic (minced) (optional)
2 C. canned tomatoes

½ C. chopped green pepper
2 T. Worcestershire sauce
1 tsp. salt
2 T. flour
2 T. oil

Dredge steak in flour and season with salt and pepper. Brown in oil and place venison steak in heavy skilelt and add remaining ingredients. Cover lightly and cook over low heat for 1½ to 2 hours. Add additional tomatoes, if necessary. Remove steak from drippings and thicken with 2 T. of flour. Serves 4.

Pot Roast ala Venison

4 lbs. venison pot roast
2½ T. flour
1 C. onion (sliced)
1½ C. canned tomatoes
½ C. water
2 cloves garlic (minced)
½ C. celery (minced)
1 T. salt

1 T. Worcestershire sauce
¼ tsp. paprika
Pinch of black pepper
¼ C. cider vinegar
1 tsp. prepared mustard
½ C. catsup
2½ T. brown sugar
¼ C. lemon juice

Dredge meat in flour. Brown in oil on all sides in heavy skillet. Place roast on rack in oven. Add tomatoes, water, garlic, vinegar, salt, and pepper. Cover and simmer for 2 hours. Combine remaining ingredients and pour over meat; cover and simmer for 1 hour or until tender. Serves 6 to 8.

Another Venison Roast

4 lbs. venison roast
3 strips bacon for larding
¼ lb. butter
½ C. water

1 tsp. lemon juice
1 C. sour cream
2 T. flour

Remove the skin and fat. Dredge in flour and sprinkle with salt and pepper. Brown venison in part of butter; put rest of butter in bottom of roaster. Lay bacon over venison meat. Roast in 350° oven until venison is tender, basting with butter and sour cream, a spoonful at a time. The roast should be pink inside and juicy. Remove roast to a hot platter. Brown flour in drippings; add water and cook for 10 minutes more. Add lemon juice, then strain. Serves 6 to 10.

NOTE: Venison may be rubbed with garlic before cooking if garlic flavor is desired. Whole onions may be placed around roast the last 20 minutes of roasting for variety.

Venison Sauce

Warm a glass of currant jelly in half as much port wine and serve hot with venison.

CURRANT JELLY SAUCE:
2 T. butter or bacon fat
3 T. flour
½ glass currant jelly (4 oz.)
1 C. water or beef stock

¼ tsp. salt
1/8 tsp. black pepper
2 T. sherry wine

Mix seasoning with flour and brown butter and flour together. Add stock of water gradually, bringing to boiling point for a few minutes. Melt currant jelly in sauce and season with 2 T. sherry wine.

North Woods Venison Loaf

1⅓ C. loosely packed bread crumbs
1½ lbs. shoulder of venison
3 T. butter
3 T. finely chopped celery
1 C. water
1¼ tsp. salt

Pepper
1 medium bay leaf marrow
1½ tsp. grated onion
1 egg (slightly beaten)
Pinch of marjoram (if desired)

Wipe meat and trim off tough tissues or fat. Remove bones and grind meat. Saute' celery in butter for 5 minutes; add bay leaf and water. Simmer for 3 minutes and discard bay leaf. Combine cooled liquid with crumbs; add meat and remaining ingredients. Mix thoroughly, then turn into greased loaf pan and bake at 350° for 1 hour. Makes 5 to 6 servings.

Farmers' Venison Stew

Meat should be marinated before mixing.

2½ lbs. shoulder of venison
1/8 tsp. pepper
3 T. shortening
1 1/8 tsp. salt
½ C. pureed tomatoes

1 medium onion (sliced)
1 T. flour
1 C. water
1 clove crushed garlic

Wipe meat, trim off any strong smelling fat. Cut into 2-inch cubes. Heat shortening and brown meat. Saute' onions and garlic in meat drippings. Add other ingredients; cover and simmer for 1-2 hours.

Venison Sausage

¼ beef meat   *¾ venison meat*

For every pound of meat, use 1 level teaspoon of Morton sausage seasoning. Mix thoroughly and grind into same container meat and seasonings were mixed. Sausage may be made into rolls and refrigerated. Slice into patties or may be stuffed into casings.

Venison Chili

1½ lbs. ground venison   *1 medium onion (chopped)*
2 cans kidney beans with liquid *1 tsp. chili powder*
1 qt. whole tomatoes   *½ tsp. paprika*
Garlic, if desired

Cook in covered pan and simmer for 2 to 3 hours.

Leg of Venison

1 (3½ to 4 lb.) leg of venison   *2 T. flour*
¼ lb. butter   *2 oz. bacon strips*
Bacon strips   *½ C. water*
1 C. sour cream

Wipe meat carefully, draw off dry skin. Lay bacon strips on lean side of leg. Salt and pepper; dredge with flour. Melt butter and add meat and cook until light brown. Place meat on a few bacon strips in pan. Roast in moderate oven for 1 hour, basting often with cream. When meat is tender, remove from pan, and add flour to drippings. Cook for 2 minutes and add water. Cook for 5 minutes; strain and serve. Serves 6.

Fried Venison Liver

1 liver of venison, cleaned,
  washed & sliced thin
1 lb. bacon
1 medium onion (sliced)

¼ C. flour
Salt and pepper
2 slices lemon

Clean and wash fresh (very fresh) liver. Slice liver and dredge in flour. Fry 4 slices bacon for drippings. Add dredge liver to hot fat and fry; add bacon slices and sliced onion. Simmer for 20 minutes, salt, and pepper, to taste. Serve with lemon slices.

Venison Sloppy Joes

1 lb. ground venison
1 can chicken gumbo soup
½ C. water

Pepper, to taste
8 T. (approx.) ketchup

Brown hamburger with onion; drain off grease. Add undiluted soup, water, pepper, and ketchup. Simmer for ½ hour. Serve on hamburger buns.

Deer Burger Hot Dish

1 lb. deerburger
1 small onion (chopped)
1 small pkg. shell macaroni
1 (No. 2) can cream-style corn

1 can chicken rice soup
Salt and pepper (to taste)
Chopped green pepper, to taste

Brown meat and onions; drain. Cook macaroni per package directions and drain. Mix all ingredients together and bake at 350° for 1 hour. Serves 4 to 6.

Moose or Reindeer Leg Roast

6 lbs. hind leg roast
¼ C. butter
4-5 sprigs parsley (minced)
½ tsp. dry savory (crumbled)
½ tsp. dried tarragon (crumbled)
1 C. red wine or part wine &
  game stock

10-12 juniper berries (crushed)
Salt and pepper
¼ C. currant jelly
½ C. red wine
1 T. brandy
1½ T. roux or flour

Melt butter; add herbs. Cook for several minutes. Place roast seasoned with salt and pepper and lightly sprinkled with flour in roasting pan. Pour butter over crust and place in preheated 450° oven. In 20 minutes reduce heat to 325°. Add wine and stock. Cover and roast for 25 minutes per pound, basting frequently. When tender, remove to heated platter and keep warm while preparing sauce. For Sauce: Add 1 C. stock to juices in roaster. Stir to loosen all bits in pan. Strain into small saucepan. Add jelly, ½ C. wine, and roux. Stir until sauce is smooth and thickened. Allow to simmer a few minutes. Pour into heated gravy boat. If juniper berries aren't found in your area, write to an herb and spice company. You can substitute equal parts of gin and stock for the wine.

Hunter's Stew

2 lbs. chuck of any big game meat
  (cut in pieces)
3 T. salad oil
2 cloves garlic (minced)
3 large onions (quartered)
1 (6 oz.) can tomato paste
1 T. flour
1 tsp. chili powder
1 tsp. oregano

1 tsp. rosemary
1½ T. seasoned salt
2 (16 oz. ea.) cans stewed
  tomatoes
½ C. snipped celery or parsley
1 C. water
3 medium carrots
½ lb. macaroni
½ C. shredded Parmesan cheese

In large Dutch oven heat salad oil and brown meat on all sides. Add garlic onion and saute' well, turning frequently. Stir in tomato paste, flour, chili powder, oregano, rosemary, seasoned salt, tomatoes, and celery or parsley. Add water and simmer, covered for 1 hour and 15 minutes. Skim off fat, if necessary. Add carrots and simmer for 45 minutes longer. Meanwhile, cook macaroni, as package directs. Drain it well and stir into stew with Parmesan cheese. Serves 6.

Venison Meat Loaf

1½-2 lbs. ground venison
¾ C. oatmeal
1 egg (beaten)
½ C. water

1½ tsp. salt
¼ tsp. pepper
¼ C. catsup
¼ C. diced onion

Microwave 8 minutes on high. Turn pan half around. Microwave for 7 minutes on High, turn, and microwave 4 minutes on High or bake in regular oven at 350° for 1½ hours.

More Meat Loaf

1½ lbs. ground meat
  (venison, moose, elk)
3 medium soft slices bread (torn)
1 C. milk
¼ C. minced onion

¼ tsp. salt
¼ tsp. each pepper, dry mustard,
  sage, celery salt, garlic salt
1 T. Worcestershire sauce

Mix all ingredients and shape into loaf. Place in baking pan. May top with ketchup. Bake at 350° for 1½ hours.

Still More Venison Meat Loaf

1 lb. ground venison
1 egg
½ C. ketchup
1 T. Worcestershire sauce

1 small onion (finely chopped)
¼ C. cracker crumbs
Bacon strips

Mix all ingredients. Bake at 350° for 45 minutes to 1 hour. Bake in pan with rack. Cover rack with foil. Place loaf on rack. Place bacon strips across meatloaf. The bacon grease will cook through meat and the really wild taste will go to bottom of pan.

(142)

Barbecued Loin

3½-4 lbs. loin
(bear, antelope, deer, elk)

Marinade

Inject roast with marinade. Heat coals to hot or gas grill on high. Salt and pepper loin and sear over coals. Reduce heat and close lid on grill. Cook for 1½ hours unless bear, then cook for 2½ hours. Serve on warmed serving platter with additional marinade added. Serve with baked potato and applesauce. Serves 6.

Deer Dip

1 lb. ground deerburger
2 lbs. Velveeta cheese
8 oz. jar hot picante sauce

1 can Golden Mushroom soup
3 cans sliced mushrooms
2-3 (4 oz. ea.) cans chopped
green chilies

Fry meat and drain any excess grease. Add all above ingredients and melt over low heat, stirring occasionally. Serve with nacho chips or corn chips.

Saddle of Venison

Wipe a 4 pound saddle of venison with damp cloth. Tie in a roll. Rub ½ tsp. pepper and 1 tsp. salt into meat. Lay in pan, add 1 T. hot fat; add 1 T. water. Roast at 400° for 1 hour. Turn, baste frequently with broth. Serve with wild rice.

Bear Loin Steaks

2 (10-inch ea.) steaks (2½ lbs.,   1½ tsp. salt
   5/8 ¾-inch thick)   ½ C. boiling water
1 T. butter or margarine (melted) Generous dash of pepper
2 tsp. lemon juice

Trim off fat because it is strong flavored. Place steak on a hot, greased broiler rack set 4 inches from heat. Combine butter and lemon juice; brush steaks. Sprinkle with half of the salt and pepper. Broil 7 to 8 minutes. Turn steaks and brush with remaining lemon butter and remaining salt and pepper. Broil another 7 to 8 minutes for well done. Remove to platter. Drizzle ½ C. water over rack and scrape the residue into the drip pan. Remove rack. Stir gravy until well blended; reheat to boiling. Pour over hot steaks and serve immediately.

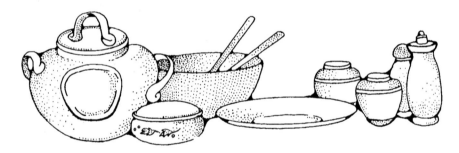

Roast Beaver

1 beaver   1 qt. water
1 tsp. baking soda   Strips of bacon
Salt   Sliced onions

Remove all surface fat from beaver. Cover meat with a weak solution of soda and water (1 tsp. soda to 1 qt. of water). Parboil by simmering gently for 10 minutes; drain. Place meat in roaster. Sprinkle with salt, cover with sliced onions, strips of bacon and roast in moderate oven (350°) until well done. Serve at once. Beaver should be cooked until the meat almost falls off the bones.

Marinated Bear Steak

Thick slice of bear loin
 (cut into steaks)
1 onion (chopped fine)
1 carrot (diced)
1 tsp. paprika
1 C. cider
1 T. lemon juice
1 clove of garlic (crushed)
1 bay leaf
¼ tsp. nutmeg

½ tsp. dry mustard
2 T. orange juice
1 clove garlic (crushed)
4 T. butter
1 tsp. prepared mustard
¼ tsp. Worcestershire sauce
½ tsp. salt
1/8 tsp. pepper
½ tsp. paprika
2 T. tomato juice

Combine the first 11 ingredients, except the meat and bring slowly to a boil. Boil for 5 minutes, then cool. Use to marinate bear steaks 24 hours in refrigerator. Remove steaks from marinade and sear on both sides in broiler under high heat. Reduce heat and broil, basting often with a mixture of the last 8 ingredients. When steaks are done, dust with salt, pepper, and parsley. Serve with mushrooms, sauteed in butter.

Bear Stew

8 lbs. bear meat
4 bags carrots
1 bag onions (No. 3 size)
1 stalk celery
1 (1½oz.) jigger vinegar

1 T. salt
1 tsp. pepper
4 (8 oz. ea.) cans mushrooms
Dash of garlic salt

Cut fat from meat. Cube meat into large pieces and brown. Clean and cut-up all vegetables and simmer meat with half of carrots, half the onions, all the celery and the vinegar. When meat and vegetables are cooked, remove carrots, celery, and onions and discard. Add remaining carrots and onions; simmer again. When done add mushrooms. Thicken stew just like you would gravy. Season to taste with salt, pepper, and garlic salt. Serves 12.

Marinade for Large Game

¾ C. salt
⅓ C. sugar
3 T. garlic salt
3 T. onion salt
3 T. celery salt
4 T. Accent
1½ oz. Tabasco sauce

¼ C. soy sauce
½ C. Worcestershire sauce
1/8 C. Kitchen Bouquet
3 C. vinegar
½ C. lemon juice
1/8 C. chablis wine
3 C. apple sauce

Place salt, sugar, garlic salt, onion salt, celery salt, and Accent in empty 1 gallon milk jug. Add 2 C. water and shake. Add Tabasco, soy, Worcestershire sauce, Kitchen Bouquet, vinegar, lemon juice, chablis wine, apple juice, and fill gallon jug with water. Use the above for needling meat. If used for marinating overnight, add 1 C. salad oil for each 3 C. of marinade. Always shake well before using. Great with any wild game and pork. (I use it to inject hind quarters of deer and antelope and pork loins.)

Venison Oriental

1 lb. venison steak
(cut in 1-inch pieces)
½ lb. mushrooms (sliced)
1 bunch green onions
(cut in 1½-inch lengths)
3 stalks celery
(cut in 1-inch pieces)

1 (8 oz.) can bamboo shoots
⅓ C. soy sauce
1 chicken bouillon cube,
dissolved in ½ C. hot water
3 large onions (sliced)
3 C. cooked rice

Brown steak. Add all ingredients, except rice. Simmer until vegetables are tender. May have to add more liquid. Serve over cooked rice.

Broiled Venison Chops
with Jelly Sauce

6-8 venison loin chops   ½ C. consomme or stock
  (1-inch to 1½-inch thick)   ¼ C. tawny port
4 T. butter   1½-2½ T. plump or red
Salt and pepper   currant jelly
1 small onion (finely minced) 2 C. sour cream
2 T. butter   (room temp.)

Preheat broiler. Spread chops with softened butter and broil for 4 to 6 minutes on a side. Salt and pepper, to taste. Saute' the minced onion in the 2 T. butter for a couple of minutes, then add wine and stock. Cover over high heat to reduce by half. Stir jelly into sour cream until blended and then stir the mixture into onions and reduced liquid; do not boil. This dish best when one person makes the sauce and another puts the chops under the broiler just 4 to 5 minutes before the sour cream and jelly are stirred into the sauce. Chops are great if grilled on outdoor grill. Be careful not to overcook meat, it becomes tough.

Tipsy Deer Chops

6 venison chips (¾-inch thick)   1 tsp. hot mustard
1 onion (finely chopped)   Dash of Worcestershire sauce
Tarragon vinegar   Chili sauce
Dash of Tabasco sauce   ½ C. bourbon whiskey

Cover chops with onion. Add vinegar to cover chops by ¼-inch in an iron skillet. Simmer until chops are tender. Combine remaining ingredients except whiskey and cook at low heat, stirring occasionally until thick. Add more vinegar or chili sauce, if needed. When the sauce is thick enough, spread generously on both sides of chops. Place in shallow pan and pour bourbon over them. Bake, uncovered at 350° for 1½ hours. Baste occasionally. Serves 3.

Salami

5 lbs. cheap hamburger (fatty) or
   deerburger (grind deer with
   beef tallow - 20%)
5 tsp. (rounded) Morton's Tender
   Quick salt

2½ tsp. each of mustard seed,
   whole coarse ground pepper
   & garlic salt
2 tsp. liquid hickory smoke
2 dashes Tabasco sauce

Mix all ingredients well and refrigerate. Knead well the next 2 days. Let set the 3rd day. Knead the fourth day and form into 2-inch rolls. Place on broiler rack and bake at 140° for 8 hours. Turn every 2 hours. (Last year we used this recipe for our deer sausage. We substituted deerburger for the hamburger and omitted the liquid smoke. On the fourth day we stuffed the sausage into 2-inch casings and put the sausage into the smokehouse for 8 hours at 140°. Can be hung or placed on racks. An oven thermometer would help to regulate the smokehouse temperature. Can be frozen for future use.)

Winter Barbecue

2 lbs. boneless venison
½ lb. bacon
1 C. chopped onion
2 cloves minced garlic
1 C. ketchup

½ C. red wine vinegar
¼ C. Worcestershire sauce
¼ C. brown sugar
Rice
Salt and pepper

Cut venison into pieces no larger than 1-inch cubes. In the bottom of a Dutch oven or large frying pan; cook bacon until crisp. Remove bacon, crumble, and set aside. In a bowl mix all ingredients, except venison and rice. Salt and pepper, to taste. Drain venison and brown it in bacon drippings. Pour off drippings and liquid; stir well. Cover tightly and simmer about 1 hour or until meat is tender, stirring occasionally. Cook rice. Serve barbecued venison on rice. Feeds 7 to 8 ordinary people.

Stuffed Chops or Loin

½ loaf dried bread
1 medium onion (chopped)
½ tsp. sage
2 tsp. butter

Salt and pepper
6 (1-inch ea.) chops from
   elk, deer, moose

Break bread into bowl. Add chopped onion, ½ tsp. sage, 2 tsp. melted butter, salt, and pepper. Mix while adding water to make sticky (not soggy). Butterfly chops or 1-inch slices of loin. Stuff chops and hold dressing in with toothpick. Sprinkle with flour and brown. Reduce heat to 350°. Add ½ C. of water; cover and cook for 1½ hours. Serve with au gratin potatoes and your favorite salad. Serves 6.

Smothered Steak

6 venison loin steaks (butterflied)
1 large green pepper (sliced)
1 large onion (sliced)

8 oz. fresh mushrooms (sliced)
Salt and pepper, to taste
6 slices provolone cheese

Cook venison steaks the way you like them, either broiled or cooked in a little oil in a skillet, seasoned to taste. In a seperate skillet, saute' peppers, onions, and mushrooms in oil or butter. Do not cook all the way done. Put steaks on a broiled pan and cover each with sauteed' vegetables and top with the provolone cheese. Place under broiler until cheese melts and just turns golden brown.

Grilled Deer Steak

6 deer loin steaks
  (cut 2-inches thick)

¼ lb. beef suet
Toothpicks

Cut meat on its side ½ to ¾ the way through horizontally. Insert beef suet. Pin meat shut with toothpicks. Grill on outdoor grill. Serves family of 4.

Venison Tenderloins

4 (1-inch ea.) thick deer loin steaks   ⅓ C. milk
1 egg   6 large soda crackers

Pound deer loin steaks to ¼-inch thick. Mix egg and milk. Beat well and roll crackers into fine crumbs. Dip loins into egg and milk mixture and then roll in cracker crumbs. Fry like normal tenderloin. Serves family of 4.

Venison Tenderloins
from Chops

Any number of loins or   Salt & pepper or garlic salt
    choice cuts from chops

Place loin on wooden cutting board and season to own liking with salt, pepper, and/or garlic salt. Tenderize with tenderizing hammer, both sides until loin is approximately ½-inch thick. The loin should now be about 5-inches to 6-inches in diameter. Cook over campfire or on grill until done. One or two of these on a bun makes a great easy burger.

Venison Roast with Apples

Venison roast   2 cooking apples (sliced)
1 C. apple juice   Salt & pepper
1 T. flour   Cooking bag

Place roast in cooking bag. Mix flour and apple juice. Salt and pepper roast. Pour juice and flour mixture over roast. Slice apples and place on roast. Bake at 350° for 1½ hours or until tender. Remove roast. Thicken gravy if needed and serve with roast.

Venison Burrito

1 (2-3 lb.) venison roast
1 pkg. taco seasoning
1 large can refried beans
1 can tomatoes & green chilies
   or jar of salsa sauce

Tortilla shells
1 onion (chopped)
Water
Grated Cheddar cheese

Rub taco seasoning into roast. Place in crock pot or roasting pan with remaining taco seasoning and cover with water. Cook on low heat for 4 to 5 hours. Check occasionally and add water if needed. Use two forks to shred meat. Then add refried beans, tomatoes, and green chile (or Salsa Ranchera) and reheat. Warm tortilla shells and spoon on meat mixture. Sprinkle with chopped onions and grated cheese and roll up and serve immediately or place in baking dish. Top with more grated cheese and tomato salsa. Return to oven on low heat for 10 to 15 minutes and serve.

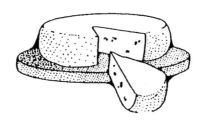

Aunt Bess's
Venison Stroganoff

Lean cuts from approximately
   4 chops or round steak
½ pkg. wide egg noodles
½ onion (sliced)

1 (12 oz.) can mushroom soup
1 (12 oz.) can dark gravy
Salt & pepper

Trim all fat and cut meat into 1-inch cubes. Brown in butter or deep fryer. Mix in skillet the meat, onion slices, mushroom soup, gravy, and 1 C. water. Salt and pepper to own liking. After contents are thoroughly heated, add noodles. Stir in, cover, and simmer with occasional stirring for approximately 1 hour.

Gravy Mix Venison Stroganoff

1 lb. venison round steak   3 pkgs. brown gravy mix
1 small can mushrooms   1 bag wide noodles

Cut steaks into small cubes, brown in 2 T. oil, and cook until done, about 20 minutes. Cut mushrooms into small pieces and add to steak. Mix gravy mixture with 3 C. water into steak and simmer for about 20 to 25 minutes. Pour over the noodles that have been boiled while the meat was cooking. Serves 3 to 4 people.

Old Fashioned Venison Stroganoff

2½ lbs. round steak   2 cans beef bouillon
  (elk, deer, antelope)   8 ozs. sour cream
1 onion (baseball size)   1/8 lbs. butter
1 (4 oz.) can mushrooms

Heat electric skillet to 375° and melt butter. Cut meat in 1-inch cubes. Slice onion and glaze in pan with mushrooms leaving water on mushrooms and glaze until water is reduced. Remove and add meat that has been rolled in flour, salt, and pepper. Brown meat, then add 2 cans bouillon and 2 cans water and reduce heat until liquid just bubbles. Simmer 3 hours covered or until liquid is reduced in half. Add onions, mushrooms, and sour cream; heat at 225° for ½ hour. Serve over Minute Rice or homemade bread. Peaches and green beans go well. Serves 6.

Roast Leg of Antelope or Venison

Wipe leg to remove all hair, sprinkle with salt and pepper; dredge with flour. Lard with strips of salt pork unless meat is fat. Roast uncovered in slow oven (300°) for 20 minutes per pound. Allow ½ pound per person.

NOTE: Some people like garlic; with knife point, make cut in leg - insert garlic clove in cut. Make about 4 to 5 cuts per leg. The last 20 minutes or roasting, sliced onion may be added around the leg.

(152)

Venison with Sherry

2 lbs. venison steak
(cut in ½-inch strips)
2 large onions
1 can sliced mushrooms
1 can golden mushroom soup

1 cube beef bouillon
½ C. water
1 oz. dry sherry
1 tsp. Worcestershire sauce
¼ lb. butter or oleo

Saute' sliced onions and mushrooms in melted butter in large skillet. Remove and set aside. Lightly brown venison in same pan. Dilute bouillon cube in water. When venison is brown add other ingredients starting with soup. Salt and pepper, to taste. Cover and simmer for 40 minutes. For a real treat serve over wild rice. If using venison chops, slice ¼-inch thick and use whole. Serves 4.

Venison Round Steak Casserole with Dumplings

1 venison round steak (cubed)
¼ C. flour
1 tsp. salt
¼ tsp. paprika

¼ tsp. pepper
Onion, to taste
2 cans cream of chicken soup
1 soup can of water

Coat meat with flour and seasonings. Brown meat and add onions and soup can of water. Bake at 350° for 40 to 45 minutes.

DUMPLINGS:
2 C. flour
4 tsp. baking powder

½ tsp. salt

Stir into these 3 ingredients ¾ C. milk and ¼ C. oil. Add 1 tsp. poultry seasoning and 1 T. celery seed. Drop mixture on roast to form dumplings. Bake for 15 to 20 minutes longer.

Venison Swiss Steak

2 lbs. round steak (¾-inch thick)   *1 clove garlic (crushed)*
½ C. flour   *1 tsp. paprika*
3 T. shortening   *1 tsp. onion salt*
1½ tsp. salt   *1 C. water*
½ tsp. pepper

Cut the steak into 6 pieces and pound the flour into the meat. Brown well in the shortening. Season with salt and pepper. Add the garlic and onion. Continue cooking until the onion is tender and browned. Add paprika, onion, salt, and water. Cover and bake in moderately hot oven (375°) until meat is tender, about 2 hours. Add more water if necessary. Serves 6.

Roast of Antelope

Clean and lard a saddle of antelope. Rub well with flour and salt and pepper. Place on rack in dry pan and roast at 300 for 2½ hours. Strips of bacon can be added on top for basting. Serve with currant jelly sauce.

Marinate antelope steaks in 1 part vinegar or lemon juice to 3 parts salad oil, 4 cloves garlic (crushed) for several hours or overnight. Remove from marinade and broil. Add garlic before broiling.

Antelope Venison

4-6 servings of round roast or
   steak (strips)
½ tsp. chili powder & Accent
2 T. butter

1½ onion (chopped)
1 can beef broth or beef bouillon
1 can golden mushroom soup
1 (4 oz.) can mushrooms

Sprinkle meat strips with Accent and chili powder. Roll in flour and brown in grease. Remove meat from skillet and drain off grease. Put butter and onion in skillet and brown. Add 2 or 3 T. flour for thickening. Stir until browned lightly. Put in beef broth soup and mushrooms. When well blended, put meat back in and simmer on low at least 1 hour, longer if you can. Add red cooking wine to sauce for fuller flavor. Serve with cooked rice or potatoes.

Braised Antelope

4 lbs. antelope
4 strips salt pork
Salt & pepper, to taste
1/8 tsp. cinnamon
1/8 tsp. cloves
⅔ C. claret or weak vinegar

½ C. water
1 bay leaf
½ onion (sliced thin)
1 C. claret or cranberry juice
1 C. milk

Trim off fat and rub with lard or salt pork. Season with salt and pepper, cinnamon, and cloves. Marinate in claret or vinegar for 2 to 3 days in a cold place. Drain and place in baking pan; add water, cover, and cook in slow oven (300°), about 1 hour. Add bay leaf, onions, and claret or cranberry juice; cover and cook until tender, about 1 hour. Remove meat and add milk to drippings. Add 1 T. of flour and stir. Heat to boiling and serve wiwth the antelope. Serve garnished with spiced apple rings.

Swiss Steak

4 lbs. deer, elk, bear meat
¾ C. chopped onions
1½ C. chopped celery
1½ C. chopped carrots

1 C. tomato sauce
1 qt. tomatoes
Salt & pepper, to taste

Brown meat in hot grease. Take out of skillet and make a thick gravy of flour and water. Add rest of ingredients and browned meat. Bake at 350° for 2 to 3 hours until vegetables are soft and sauce is thick.

Antelope or Venison

4-6 servings or round roast or
   steak (strips)
½ tsp. chili powder & Accent
2 T. butter

1½ onion (chopped)
1 can beef broth or beef bouillon
1 can golden mushroom soup
1 (4 oz.) can mushrooms

Sprinkle meat strips with Accent and chili powder. Roll in flour and brown in grease. Remove meat from skillet and drain off grease. Put butter and onion in skillet and brown. Add 2 or 3 T. flour for thickening. Stir until browned lightly. Put in beef broth soup and mushrooms. When well blended, put meat back in and simmer on low at least 1 hour, longer if you can. Add red cooking wine to sauce for fuller flavor. Serve with cooked rice or potatoes.

Steak Roll Ups

1½-2 lbs. venison round steak
1 large white onion (diced)
1 lb. smoked bacon
Garlic salt

Oregano
2 (4 oz. ea.) cans mushrooms
Quick-mixing flour

Cut the venison steak into pieces approximately 4-inches by 3-inches. Hammer the pieces with a meat tenderizing tool until the size is approximately 6x4-inches. Layer the diced onion and 2 strips of uncooked bacon in the middle of each piece of meat. Sprinkle garlic salt and oregano sparginly on top of the bacon. Roll each piece into a bundle and secure with twine. Brown each bundle in a frying pan and then place in a Dutch oven. Add ¾ C. of water to the frying pan and scrape the pan. Then pour the contents over the meat in the Dutch oven. Simmer, covered, for about 3 hours, adding water if necessary. Remove the meat to heated platter and add mushrooms and quick-mixing flour to the Dutch oven to thicken the juices. Ladle the gravy over the meat and serve with wild rice. Serves 4.

Braised Antelope

4 lbs. antelope
4 strips salt pork
Salt & pepper, to taste
1/8 tsp. cinnamon
1/8 tsp. cloves
⅔ C. claret or weak vinegar

½ C. water
1 bay leaf
½ onion (sliced thin)
1 C. claret or cranberry juice
1 C. milk

Trim off all fat and rub with lard or salt pork. Season with salt and pepper, cinnamon, and cloves. Marinate in claret or vinegar for 2 to 3 days in a cold place. Drain and place in baking pan; add water, cover, and cook in slow oven (300°) about 1 hour. Add bay leaf, onion, claret or cranberry juice; cover and cook until tender, about 1 hour. Remove meat and add milk to drippings. Add 1 T. of flour and stir. Heat to boiling and serve with the antelope. Serve garnished with spiced apple rings.

Bold Charcoal Steak

12 ozs. beer	¼ tsp. liquid smoke
½ C. chili sauce	½ C. chopped onion
½ C. cooking oil	2 cloves garlic (minced)
2 T. soy sauce	3 lbs. venison steak
1 T. prepared mustard	1 tsp. salt
½ tsp. Tabasco sauce	½ tsp. pepper

In saucepan, mix all ingredients except steak, salt, and pepper. Simmer for 30 minutes. Brush meat well with sauce. Cook over charcoal briquettes for 20 to 30 minutes per side or until well done, basting frequently with sauce. Season both sides of steaks with salt and pepper during last few minutes of cooking. Serves 6.

Venison Mince Meat

MUST BE DONE IN ORDER LISTED:

2 lbs. lean venison (cooked tender & put through food chopper)	1 T. salt
	2 c. brown sugar
½ lb. suet (chopped fine)	1 qt. sweet cider
5 lbs. apples (chopped fine)	1 C. meat stock

Allow the above mixture to come to a boil. Simmer for 1 hour, stirring occasionally. To this mixture add in order:

2½ pts. grape juice	1 C. molasses
1 tsp. mace	1 orange (juice & peel, chopped fine)
½ tsp. pepper	
2 tsp. allspice	1 lemon (juice & peel, chopped fine)
2 tsp. cloves	
2 tsp. nutmeg	¾ C. vinegar
2 tsp. cinnamon	

Allow entire mixture to come to a boil and boil for 10 minutes. Pack in sterile jars to within 1-inch of top. Put on caps, screw band firmly to tighten. Process pints 25 minutes, quarts 25 minutes at 10 lbs. pressure. Yields: 10 pints.

"Early Days" Boiled Heart

Heart of deer, elk, etc.   *Bay leaf if available*
Salt & pepper

Put heart in pot large enough to cover heart with water. Salt and pepper, to taste and add bay leaf. Bring to a boil and then simmer for about 1 hour. Let cool after done. Slice in thin pieces and use as lunch meat or serve for snacks.

Barbecued Ribs

Your favorite barbecue sauce *Venison ribs*

Prepare ribs as you would for baking, then remove ribs by cutting on inside of rib bone and peeling meat around ribs. Cut meat in strips; marinate rib meat in barbecue sauce overnight. Put meat in pint jars and can. (NOTE: Do not add salt to meat as there is enough in the sauce.) Process pints 75 minutes; quarts 90 minutes at 10 lbs. pressure.

Good Old Fried Liver

Soak liver in salt water to help remove all blood. Slice liver into pieces about 3/8-inch thick and return to clean salt water. While slicing clean liver of all fat and tough veins, etc. In large skillet heat grease and slice two or three large onions cooking until onions are about half done. At this time drain liver and roll in flour seasoned with salt and pepper. As soon as liver is coated add to the hot grease. Push all of the onions to one side stirring occasionally. Cook liver quickly but not too long. Liver has its best taste when still slightly pink or just past that stage. (In my opinion most liver is ruined because it is cooked too long.)

Sweet and Sour Venison

2 lbs. venison (cubed)
2 T. hot shortening
2 beef bouillon cubes
1 (1 lb. 4½ oz.) can pineapple
  chunks
¼ C. brown sugar
Hot rice

2 T. cornstarch
¼ C. vinegar
1 T. soy sauce
1 medium green pepper
  (cut in strips)
¼ C. onion (thin sliced)

Brown venison slowly in hot shortening. Add 1 C. water, bouillon cubes, and ¼ tsp. salt; mix well. Cover and simmer until tender, about 1 hour. Meanwhile, drain pineapple, save syrup. Combine brown sugar and cornstarch; add pineapple syrup, vinegar, soy sauce, and ½ tsp. salt. Cook and stir over medium-high heat until thickened and bubbly. Remove from heat. Add sauce to venison and mix well. Stir in pineapple, green pepper, and onion. Cook over low heat for 2 to 3 minutes or until vegetables are tender-crisp. Serve over rice. Makes 6 servings.

Venison Paprika With Noodles

2 lbs. venison steak (cubed)
3 T. shortening
1 T. paprika
1 tsp. salt

1/8 tsp. pepper
1/8 tsp. garlic salt
1 C. water
1 pkg. noodles

Melt shortening in skillet and cook meat until brown. Season with paprika, salt, pepper, and garlic salt; add water. Cover and simmer for 1 hour or until venison is tender. Prepare noodles as directed on package. Arrange meat on noodles. Reserve meat juice and serve separately as a sauce.

Chicken Fried Venison Steak

1 C. flour
1 tsp. salt
¼ tsp. pepper

Venison round steak
Oil

Tenderize steak in portion size pieces. Roll or shake steak in mixture of flour, salt, and pepper. Put oil in skillet 1/8-inch deep. Heat skillet over moderate temperature. Place steak in skillet to brown both sides. Remove steak and place in baking dish. Bake at 350° for 25 to 30 minutes. Serve.

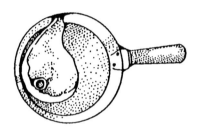

Deer Pepper Steak

1 lb. deer round steak
½ C. soy sauce
1 clove garlic
1½ tsp. grated fresh ginger or
  ½ tsp. ground ginger
¼ C. salad oil
2 tomatoes (cut into wedges)

1 C. green onion (sliced)
1 C. red or green peppers
  (cut in 1-inch squares)
2 stalks celery (sliced)
1 T. cornstarch
1 C. water

Cut round steak while still frozen into thin strips. Combine soy sauce, garlic, and ginger; add deer. Toss and set aside while preparing vegetables. Heat oil in large frying pan or wok. Add deer and toss over high heat until browned. Add vegetables. Toss until vegetables are tender-crisp, about 10 minutes. Mix cornstarch with water. Add to pan, stir, and cook until thickened. Add tomatoes and heat; serve with rice.

Spicy Venison Strips

1½ lbs. venison steak (¼-inch thick)
2 T. butter
1 T. instant minced onion
Pinch of cayenne pepper
¼ tsp. chili powder
¼ tsp. ground celery seed
1 T. ground pepper

1 C. beef broth or 2 beef
   bouillon cubes
1 C. boiling water
1 clove garlic (minced)
½ tsp. salt
¼ tsp. ground cinnamon

Cut steaks into strips. Brown in hot butter in large skillet. Combine remaining ingredients; add meat. Stir to mix. Cover and simmer for 25 to 30 minutes or until meat is fork tender. Serve immediately over rice, mashed potatoes or noodles. Serves 5 to 6.

Venison Sub Gum

1 lb. venison steak
1 T. paprika
2 T. butter
¼ tsp. garlic powder
1½ C. water and 2 bouillon cubes
   for broth
1 C. green onions (sliced 1-inch;
   1 bunch)

2 green peppers (chunks)
2 celery stalks (diced)
2 T. cornstarch
¼ C. water
¼ C. soy sauce
2 large firm tomatoes (chunks)
3 C. cooked rice (hot)
Chinese noodles

Cut steak into 1/8-inch strips across the grain. Sprinkle meat with paprika. Brown meat and butter in skillet; add garlic and broth. Cover and simmer for 45 to 60 minutes. Stir in onions, green pepper chunks, and diced celery. Cover and cook for 5 more minutes. Blend cornstarch, water, and soy sauce. Stir into meat mixture and stir until clear and thickened. Add tomato chunks and stir gently. Serve over rice and sprinkle with Chinese noodles. Serves 4.

Oven Barbecued Venison Ribs

4 lbs. venison ribs
1 T. butter
1 clove garlic
½ C. catsup
⅓ C. chili sauce
2 T. brown sugar
2 T. chopped onions

1 T. Worcestershire sauce
1 T. prepared mustard
1 tsp. celery salt
¼ tsp. salt
Dash of hot pepper sauce
2 T. Real Lemon juice

Simmer cut-up in enough salt water to cover until nearly tender, about 1 hour. In saucepan, melt butter. Add clove of garlic (crushed) and cook 4 to 5 minutes. Add the rest of the ingredients and bring to a boil. Drain ribs, place in shallow pan, pour boiling sauce over ribs. Bake at 350° for 20 minutes or until tender, basting often with sauce. Serves 6 to 8.

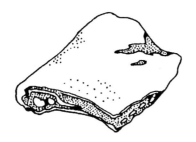

Sauteed Venison

1 lb. venison (well-trimmed)
1 C. flour
1 T. dried minced onion

Cooking oil
Salt & pepper, to taste

Cut venison into pieces about 3/8-inch thick and 1½-inch square. Dredge pieces in flour seasoned with salt and pepper. In heavy skillet, add 1/8-inch good cooking oil and heat on medium-high. Add onion evenly to hot oil and as soon as it begins to brown add the pieces of venison. Cook about 3 minutes or until juices appear on top side of meat. Turn and cook approximately 3 minutes and serve immediately. As this uses thin pieces of meat, be very careful to not overcook.

Breakfast Venison Hash

Leftover venison stew   *Velveeta cheese*

Using venison stew leftovers, if any, or make a whole new batch - mash, mix and stir stew ingredients until well blended. Drain off excess liquid. Fry in a buttered Teflon pan until warmed through and browned on the outside, turning once or twice. Just before serving, add a few slices of Velveeta cheese and you have all you need for breakfast.

Charcoal Grilled Venison

Venison roast or steak   *Toothpicks*
Bacon

Trim venison of any fat. Wrap bacon strips around venison securing with toothpicks until entire piece of meat is wrapped with one layer of bacon. Cook over a good bed of coals until center of meat is reddish-pink (be sure not to overcook venison, a 1-inch to 1½-inch thick roast should take between 20 and 30 minutes). The bacon adds flavor, juice and keeps the meat from burning. Enjoy!

Steak and Wild Rice

1½ lbs. steak (venison or beef)   *1 can cream of mushroom soup*
1½ T. oil   *½ C. dry sherry*
2 large onions (ringed)   *1½ tsp. garlic salt*
1 can sliced mushrooms   *3 C. cooked wild rice*
* (drain & reserve juice)*

Cut steak in thin strips and brown in oil. Add onions andn saute' until tender. Blend soups, sherry, mushroom juice, and garlic salt. Pour over steak and add mushrooms. Reduce heat and cover; simmer for 1 hour. Serve over bed of wild rice.

Venison Steak with Morel Mushrooms

2-4 frozen venison steaks
4 qts. washed morel mushrooms
  (less may be used)

2 T. butter
Salt & pepper, to taste
Oil for frying

Thaw venison steaks. If from an old deer, steaks should be marinated in a tenderizer and pounded until tender. Brown steaks on each side, in a large iron pan or on a griddle. Add thoroughly washed morels. The mushrooms may have to be washed four times to remove sand and other matter. Lower heat and simmer with salt, pepper, and butter until steaks are tender.

Stuffed Cabbage Rolls

12 large cabbage leaves
1½ lbs. ground bear meat
  or shredded venison
1 beaten egg
½ C. milk
¼ C. finely chopped onion
1 tsp. Worcestershire sauce
Ground pepper

1½ C. cooked rice
1 (10¾ oz.) can condensed
  tomato soup
1 T. brown sugar
1 T. lemon juice
2 T. chopped dill
1 T. garlic salt

In mixing bowl combine egg, milk, onion, Worcestershire sauce, pepper, garlic, and salt; mix well. Add ground meat and cooked rice; mix thoroughly. Immerse leaves in boiling water until limp, about 3 minutes; drain. Place ⅓ C. meat mixture on each large leaf; fold in sides. Starting at bottom of leaf, roll-up each leaf making sure folded sides are included in roll. Arrange in a 12x7½x2-inch baking pan. Stir together condensed tomato soup, brown sugar, dill, and lemon juice; pour sauce mixture over cabbage rolls. Bake, uncovered at 350° for 1¼ hours, basting once or twice with sauce. Serves 6.

(165)

Buffalo

1 (12 lb.) rump of buffalo	*½ tsp. marjoram*
2 strips salt pork	*1 tsp. salt*
2 cloves garlic (crushed)	*Black pepper*
½ tsp. thyme	*1 bottle red wine*

Cut roast in 2 pieces. Cut slit and insert 1 strip of salt pork in each. Tie together. Mix other ingredients and marinate 24 hours in refrigerator. Remove from marinade. In roasting pan, slice onions to cover bottom, lay roast on top of onions. Pour 2½ cups of water with 3 beef bouillon cubes dissolved in. Cover roaster and roast at 325° for 4 hours, basting every 30 minutes. Drain; add 1 C. sherry, 2 T. tomato paste, salt, and pepper. Baste and bake for 20 minutes longer, uncovered. Remove roast from roaster and place on platter — add flour to broth for gravy. Precook vegetables. Arrange around roast and serve with gravy.

Buffalo Roast with Sweet Potatoes

6 lbs. rump roast of buffalo	*6 sweet potatoes*
1 recipe of marinade	*½ C. maple syrup*

Remove fat and lard from roast. Marinate in any marinade for 24 hours. Wipe dry and save marinade. Brown meat for 20 minutes in hot oiled skillet. Add the marinade and 1 T. tomato paste. Bake at 350° for 2½ hours. Baste every 30 minutes. Meanwhile, cook sweet potatoes and heat maple syrup. Remove roast from roaster or pan and slice. From broth make gravy. Arrange roast on platter with mapled sweet potatoes around slices of roast. Drizzle gravy over meat.

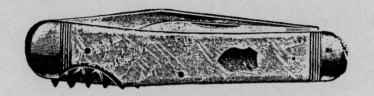

OUTDOOR
COOKIN'

Index

Hot To Keep Bacon From Molding

Bacon   *Clean cloth*
Vinegar

Bacon, regardless of the weather, molds very easily. With the mold it becomes rancid and loses its good flavor entirely. To prevent bacon from molding, take a clean cloth and wash the bacon with vinegar. This will not only prevent it from molding but makes it retain its good fresh taste.

Poached Stuff

8 English muffins   *16 slices Canadian bacon*
8 slices American cheese   *8 eggs*

Toast English muffins and fry Canadian bacon while poaching eggs. Place Canadian bacon on muffins. Cover with cheese and top with poached egg. Quick and easy in camp. Serves 4.

Camp Breakfast

1 fresh liver (deer, elk, antelope)   *1 green pepper (chopped)*
1 onion (chopped)   *Salt & pepper*
6 eggs   *Frying oil*

Peel skin off fresh liver; soak in salt water overnight. Cut liver into small pieces. Put liver, chopped onion, and green pepper into frying pan (large) and fry until liver is well done. Add eggs and stir until eggs are cooked. Salt and pepper, to own taste.

Rubies

1 lb. sausage	4 slices cheese
1 lb. bacon	Flour, salt & pepper
4 hash brown patties	¼ medium onion (chopped)
8 eggs	4 slices American cheese
2 C. milk	

Make sausage gravy with sausage, milk, salt and pepper by mixing milk, 2 T. flour, salt, and pepper and adding to browned sausage with most of grease poured off; set aside and keep warm. Fry bacon and hash browns and cover with cheese. Make 2 egg-onion omelet by placing the eggs, onion in cup and beating and pouring in pan and turning once. Put hash browns on plate and cover with gravy. Lay omelet over hash browns. Serve with bacon on side with milk. Serves 4. Big breakfast for a snowed in day. Takes quite awhile to make.

Dutch Oven Egg Casserole

½ lb. bacon	1 dozen eggs
½ lb. sausage	6 slices bread
1 (4 oz.) can stem & pieces	¼ green pepper (minced)
mushrooms	3 ozs. Velveeta cheese
1 medium onion	(1½-inch cubes)

Cut bacon in small pieces and fry in Dutch oven with sausage until done. Pour off most of grease and add mushrooms and onion, stirring frequently. Cook until onions are glazed. In bowl, mix eggs and broken up bread, salt, pepper, green pepper, and cut-up cheese. Add directly to Dutch oven. Put on lid and cook at 375° for 1 hour or place in coals of campfire being sure to place some coals on top for 1 hour. Will be golden brown on top. Serve with toast and jelly. Serves 6 hunters or fishermen.

Quick Stroganoff

1 qt. canned venison
½ C. chopped onion
3 C. dry noodles
3 T. tomato juice

1 T. pepper
2 tsp. Worcestershire sauce
1 (8 oz.) carton sour cream

In Dutch oven, shred canned venison. Add onion and dry noodles. Mix and add tomato juice, pepper, and Worcestershire sauce. Swing over low coals, cover, and simmer for 30 minutes; add sour cream. Reheat a few minutes and serve. You can cook on top of stove but cooking over a wood fire adds extra flavor to this easy dish.

Stove Top Baked Beans

1 (31 oz.) can pork & beans
6 ozs. American cheese (cubed)
¼ C. Minute Rice
1 T. mustard

¼ C. brown sugar (packed)
¼ C. catsup
1 tsp. dried minced onion

Combine all ingredients in 2-quart saucepan. Cook over medium-low heat for approximately 1 hour, stirring occasionally. If cooking over a campfire, watch that hot spots don't scorch the cheese. Serves 6.

Dutch Oven Stew

2 lbs. venison round steak
2 onions (cut in large chunks)
3 stalks celery (sliced)
1 tsp. salt

3 potatoes (cubed)
4 carrots (sliced)
2 tsp. pepper
¼ C. oil

Large campfire. Dig hole large enough for Dutch oven. Brown venison in Dutch oven with oil. Add all other ingredients. Drop biscuits on top. Put lid on. Put 2 shovelsful of coals in hole. Place Dutch oven on top of coals. Cover with rest of coals and dirt. Leave buried 4 to 5 hours.

V-8 Camp Roast

1 (3-4 lb.) venison roast
2 medium onions
1½ (12 oz. ea.) cans V-8 cocktail juice

3 medium potatoes
4 large carrots
Salt & pepper

Trim all fat. Brown roast in skillet with butter. Quarter onion, potatoes, and carrot. Combine all vegetables and meat in Dutch oven or cast iron pot. Season to liking with salt and pepper. Pour in enough V-8 juice to cover contents. Put Dutch oven with lid in campfire coals or on rack above fire. In coals works better. Cook until meat falls apart with fork. Usually if put on the fire in mid to late afternoon, it will be ready after the evening hunt.

Venison Barbecue Sandwich

2 lbs. venison round steak
½ lb. bacon
1 C. chopped onion
2 cloves garlic (minced)
1 C. ketchup

½ C. red wine vinegar
¼ C. Worcestershire sauce
¼ C. brown sugar
Salt & pepper
12 buns

Slice venison round steak in 1/8-inch strips 4-inches long. In bottom of Dutch oven cook bacon until crisp. Remove, crumble, and set aside. In a bowl mix all ingredients, except venison. Salt and pepper, to taste. Brown venison in bacon drippings and pour off grease. Add bowlful of ingredients to venison; stir well. Cover tightly and simmer for 1 hour or until tender, stirring occasionally. Serve in buns with extra sauce. Can cook in fire over low coals or on Coleman Stove. Serves 6.

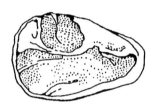

Suet Pudding

1½ C. kidney suet (beef)
5 C. flour
Salt & pepper
2 lbs. sirloin or round steak
  (venison is good, too)

1 good sliced onion
1 old dish towel or diaper
1 string

Mix flour and suet. Add 1 tsp. salt and 1 tsp. pepper and add water to make dough. Cut-up meat in 1-inch squares and chop onion. Spread dough about 1-inch thick on towel or diaper and place meat and onion in middle. Pull dough up around meat until completely covered and tie with string making several rounds to secure. Place in boiling pot with plate upside down in bottom and cover with water with 1 tsp. salt added. Boil for 4 hours, turning once. Remove from cloth by cutting string. Slice and serve covered with juice. Serve with bread and butter and burgundy wine. Serves 6.

Camp Pie

10 potatoes
2 ozs. butter
Milk, salt & pepper
1 can mushroom soup

1½ lbs. ground venison
1 can peas
1 can corn
1 (4 oz.) can mushrooms

Boil 10 potatoes and mash with milk and butter, salt and pepper. Butter Dutch oven and line with ¾ of potatoes. Place in oven and brown. Mix meat, peas, corn, mushrooms, salt, and pepper. Be sure and drain vegetables. Add to Dutch oven and cover with layer of mashed potatoes. Spread butter on top and bake for 1 hour or until brown on top. Serve with whatever is left in camp. Serves 6. Good last day in camp to get rid of what's left. Don't be afraid to add whatever is left in camp to the pie.

Spicy Red Snapper

2 lbs. red snapper
⅓ C. steak sauce
¼ C. melted fat or oil

1 T. vinegar
1 tsp. salt
½ tsp. curry powder

Cut into serving size portions. Combine remaining ingredients and mix thoroughly. Place fish, skin side up, on well-greased foil and brush with sauce on both sides. Bring the foil up over the food and close all edges with tight double folds. Make 6 packages. Place on hot coals. Cook for 45 to 60 minutes or until fish flakes easily with a fork. Yields: 6 servings.

Camp Fish in Foil

8 fillets of walleye,
   smallmouth bass
4 C. cooked Minute Rice
Juice of 1 lemon
¼ lb. butter

Garlic salt
Seasoned salt
Pepper
2 medium onions

Mix melted butter with juice of 1 lemon. Cross 2 pieces of 18-inch foil per person. Place onion slices on foil and salt and pepper. Place fillet on onions and sprinkle with seasoned salt and garlic salt. Cover with rice and lemon juice. Put several pats of butter on rice. Cover with onion and second fillet, season fish and pour juice and butter over top. Seal foil and place in coals of fire for 40 minutes. Slit top and let fish get brown and serve. Serves 4.

Campfire Broil

3 lbs. pan-dressed small fish
2 tsp. salt
Dash of pepper

⅓ C. chopped onion
⅓ C. chopped parsley
3 strips bacon (cut in half)

Clean, wash, and dry fish. Prepare 6 pieces of heavy-duty aluminum foil, 12x12-inches each. Grease lightly. Divide fish into 6 portions. Place fish on foil. Sprinkle with salt and pepper. Place onion and parsley on fish. Top with bacon. Bring the foil up over the food and close all edges with tight folds. Make 6 packages. Place packages on a grill about 4-inches from hot coals. Cook for 10 to 15 minutes or until fish flakes easily when tested with a fork.

Notes

OTHER
STUFF

Helpful Hints

When you fry chicken, it will brown much better if you dry the pieces before flouring.

To freshen coconut, soak it in sweet milk for a few minutes.

Thaw frozen fish in milk to remove the frozen taste and make fish taste fresher.

Soaking fish in vinegar and water before cooking also freshens and adds a sweet tender taste.

To prevent spattering and to keep sausage links from shrinking, dip or roll them in flour before frying.

Don't ruin fresh fish by cooking to fast or at too high of temperature.

Put 1 T. butter in potatoes, macaroni, and noodles to keep from boiling over.

To cut the smell of grease when frying fish or chicken put ½ tsp. peanut butter in the pan. Peanut butter will leave no taste.

Vinegar in water, when boiling eggs, will keep them from cracking.

Salt in the water when boiling eggs will make them peel easier.

To avoid spattering of fat in frying meats, sprinkle a little salt in the bottom of pan.

Try cooking rice in liquids other than water-apple juice, orange juice, tomato juice, bouillon or milk.

For black frosting for party cupcakes, add blue food coloring to your favorite chocolate frosting.

To make garlic butter, peel and slice a clove of garlic. Place in a bowl with ¼ C. of butter. Cover tightly and let stand for 1 hour. Remove garlic.

When making jelly or jams, put 1 tsp. butter in the jars to prevent foam from forming.

When making rolled cookies, roll them out on powdered sugar instead of flour and they won't get tough.

To keep soft cookies soft, put a piece of bread in the cookie jar with the cookies.

When cracking nuts, freeze before you crack them. The goodies come out whole.

To soften brown sugar, put in a jar with a piece of moist paper towel under the lid or heat sugar in the oven for several minutes.

To see if your old yeast is still good, put 1 tsp. in a cup of warm water and add 1 T. sugar. If it foams and rises in 10 minutes it is still good for baking.

Rub chicken with lemon, instead of washing, it cleans and flavors too.

Prevent banana slices from turning brown by brushing lightly with lemon juice.

Bake stuffed peppers in a tube pan and they won't fall over while baking.

To soften marshmallows put them in the refrigerator.

When baking fruit pies, avoid bubble-overs by standing a piece of uncooked macaroni in a slash in the top crust. This acts as a safety valve.

When measuring molasses, first dip your measuring cup into flour and the molasses will not stick.

Fresh eggs are rough and chalky in appearance, old eggs are smooth and shiny.

To make your plastic wrap cling, moisten the rim of your bowl or container.

Don't burn your fingers with too-short matches when you light candles use a piece of uncooked spaghetti.

When milk goes bad, use in pancakes, waffles and other morning delicacies. Can make a sour milk cake.

If your cheese dries out, simply grate and use in recipes that call for grated cheese.

Old bananas? Don't pitch them, make banana bread and use the peeling to polish your silver.

Before following a recipe from a cookbook, slip the open book into a clear plastic food storage bag. Keeps the whole book clean.

Make cookie cutters from the metal edges of foil and wax paper boxes. They can be easily bent into unusual shapes to please the children.

If the juice from fruit pies runs over in the oven, put salt on it. This causes the juice to burn to a crisp and is easier to remove.

To prevent splashing when frying meat, sprinkle a little salt into the pan before putting the fat in.

Sweeten whipped cream with powdered sugar if dessert serving maybe delayed whip stays fully longer than when granulated sugar is used.

Rub dry mustard on your hands after peeling onions, and then wash in the ordinary way. You will find that all odor will be removed.

To remove rain spots from satin, felt and similar materials. Use a soft ball of tissue paper. Rub the affected parts with a circular movement.

Before adding raisins or currants to the batter for cakes or muffins, heat them in a dish over low heat or hot water until they are very warm. This will prevent them from sinking to the bottom of the cake or muffins.

Too much salt in gravy or soup may be remedied by adding a quartered white potato and boiling for 10 minutes.

Freeze leftover pancakes separately between pieces of waxed paper. For hurry up breakfasts, simply pop pancakes into toaster or microwave oven and serve hot with your favorite syrup.

When making jam, rub the bottom of the pan with butter. This prevents burning and keeps the jam clear.

Peel onions under running water and they will not irrate eyes.

When a recipe calls for a quantity of melted butter take care to measure the butter after melting.

Measure a cupful of whipped cream after it is whipped.

If egg yolks become stringy after being added to hot puddings, especially tapioca, use a beater; the lumps will adhere to the beater, and leave the pudding smooth.

Whether cooking eggs on top of the range or in the oven, always use low or moderate and even heat. If cooked at too high a temperature, eggs become tough. If adding hot liquids to beaten eggs, add just a little at a time.

When soft custard separates on removal from the stove, beat it hard for 5 minutes with an egg beater.

When celery loses its crispness, place it in a pan of cold water. Slice a raw potato and put it in the pan. Let stand for a few hours. Remove the celery from the water and you will find that it has regained its original crispness.

If you run out of baking powder when you need some, use 2 level teaspoons cream of tartar to 1 teaspoon soda. This is the equivalent of 4 teaspoons of baking powder.

If you run out of powdered sugar, put granulated sugar in blender and blend until real fine.

Save those milk jugs; try storing sugar in a clean dry one, the sugar will not harden as it does in the bag.

When making jelly, just shave paraffin right into sterilized glasses. The hot jelly will melt the paraffin and will rise to the top and harden as the jelly cools.

If you like beans, but they don't like you, put a pinch of ground ginger in the beans when cooking them. Just a pinch will do the trick.

Egg shells contain valuable nutrients for your plants. Save egg shells, soak them for a day or so in a lidded container of water, then treat your plants to this fertilizing drink.

If you go on a picnic and forget the bottle opener for the soft drinks, use your seat-beat buckle will pry those caps right off.

When cooking over an open campfire, coat the bottom and sides of the pot with soap. It's the soap that gets black not the pot.

When traveling always carry all prescription drugs in their original containers. If planning to gone a long time take an extra prescription with you.

Oatmeal bath is a tonic for dry skin, put a quarter of cup of old-fashioned oatmeal into a nylong stocking foot and tie end. Run a shallow tubful of very hot water and drop the 2 oatmeal bags in. Let them set for 15 or 20 minutes. When ready to take bath, run rest of your water. Makes your skin feel soft and not tight, dried-out sensation.

Here is how to bandage the tip of the finger so it will stay. Make a lengthwise cut down the center of each adhesive end, cutting only as far as the pad. Remove the paper backing and cover the cut as usual. Then cross the half-strips at each end, so the bandage is secured by an X.

Keep a bay leaf in the flour cannister to keep the flour dry during humid months.

Brown sugar will stay soft forever if the box is wrapped tightly in a plastic bag and stored in the freezer.

Cracked eggs don't have to be discarded. Just be sure to use them in recipes in which they are completely cooked.

Plastic mesh bags in which onions are sold, make "free" scouring pads.

When there's a crowd coming, the tops and bottoms of egg cartons can be used as extra ice trays.

For more chocolaty cakes and brownies, dust the greased pans with cocoa powder mixed with the flour.

A plastic ketchup or mustard dispenser filled with frosting can be substituted for a frosting bag and tip.

Thaw fish in milk for a "fresh-caught" taste.

To prevent your salt shaker from clogging, place 5 to 10 grains of rice inside.

When chopping onions, cut the root end off last to shed less tears.

To separate an egg use a small funnel.

Cleaning Hints

To remove blood stains, wet stain, sprinkle with meat tenderizer, scrub, and wash.

To remove carpet stain, sprinkle salt, and let salt absorb stain and vacuum. If stain isn't dried in.

Instead of bowl cleaner drop in 2 denture cleaner tablets. Let dissolve, brush, and flush.

Hardwater spots or rust in dishwasher or on dishes add 1 tsp. powdered orange breakfast drink to your detergent each time you run machine. Dishes look beautiful.

Sprinkle baking soda on oven spills while still hot, let cool, and brush out.

Oven racks are just as hard to clean as your outdoor grill! But they don't have to be. Just apply a version of this little trick. Soak the racks in your bathtub. Just fill the tub with water, add dishwasher brand detergent and a little white vinegar to cut the grease. Put your feet up for an hour while that dirt and grime soaks away! Rinse and presto!

To clean shower head, try boiling it once a month in a mild solution of white vinegar and water.

To shine your stove after cleaning and scrubbing with scouring powders. Try a little liquid car polish and a damp cloth to brighten the enamel or metal.

To polish chrome just take a small sheet of aluminum foil, turn the shiny side out. Dampen the chrome with water and polish with the foil. As you polish, it will turn black, but wipe with cloth and will shine like new.

To prevent lime deposits from building up in your humidifier, drop an old copper scouring pad into the water container.

To clean venetian blinds, hang the blinds in the shower, turn on the water and let the shower do the work.

For sticky locks apply a little talcum powder.

To clean outside grill rack, place in garbage can and cover with industrial strength detergent, fill can with water and soak overnight. Hose off the next morning.

To remove wrinkles from velvets and velours, place in a medium dryer with 2 or 3 damp towels and spin away wrinkles. (Never iron - it spoils the pile.)

To clean canvas sandals and casual shoes, spray with carpet cleaner and brush lightly with a toothbrush. Let dry and brush again.

To get rid of him lines when lengthening blue jeans, take a blue crayon and color over hemline. Cover ironing board with newspaper or cloth, and iron in crayon color by pressing the jeans wrong-side-out.

To get that spot out in permanent press, simply rub with a little white toothpaste on the stain and rinse. Repeat until the stain is out.

To buff up your plastic plates and glasses with scratches and discoloring, use toothpaste and an old toothbrush and rinse with warm water.

When changing the water in your fresh-water aquarium use the water to water your houseplants. This fishy water is rich in everything they need.

Make your own fabric softener sheet by dabbing liquid softener on a wash cloth and throw in dryer as you would a sheet of bought softener.

To make white shoes look whiter cover scuffs use white typewriter correcting fluid. Just white out the scuff and polish.

For silver and gold shoes use an old toothbrush and tooth polish.

Tar on car can be removed by making a paste of baking soda and appling gently with a sponge. That hard to remove tar will come right off.

To remove crease from lengthening clothes, try a little white vinegar. Dampen the crease liberally with vinegar and place a damp cloth over crease and press with a hot iron.

To touch up shabby cuffs and waists in sweaters, dip them into hot water, blot excess water with a towel and dry with hot air from a blow dryer. They'll shrink back to size and make the sweater look fresh again.

To remove scuff from light colored shoes use a gum eraser. The kind you use in school.

If you run out of fabric softener use a little cream rinse.

Nail polish remover will remove crayon marks on windows and woodwork.

Keep a wet sponge handy when ironing, to dampen spots that have dried out.

The mark often left on a garment that has been cleaned with benzine can be prevented if the material is ironed under a damp cloth immediately after cleaning.

Table salt and cream of tartar, equal parts, will remove rust stains. Wet the spot and spread the mixture on thickly, then place the material in the sun.

When white furs need cleaning, spread them on a clean cloth dampened with alcohol, then run French chalk into the hair and roll the fur up in a cloth for a couple of days. Then comb until every bit of chalk is combed out. Or, it may be cleaned by rubbing equal parts of salt and flour well into the roots and then shaking out.

Egg stains on washable materials may be removed by soaking the garment in cold water for a short time before washing will soap and water in the usual way.

Never put hot water on milk and cream stains. Wash them in cold water, followed by soap and water. Rinse in clear water.

To clean hands from vegetable stains, rub with a slice of raw potato.

To remove tea, coffee, or cocoa stains, use glycerine. A fresh stain can be removed by gentle rubbing; if the stain is old, soak in glycerine for sometime.

Dishes that have become brown from baking, may have the stain removed by soaking in strong borax and water.

After polishing white shoes, rub over them with a piece of wax paper. This prevents the polish from rubbing off on your clothes and hands. Especially good for baby's shoes.

When cleaning windows add vinegar to the water and dry with old newspapers.

Plastic drinking glasses and cups often come with a price sticker glued to the surface. If you soak them in hot water the paper will come off, but glue remains. Sprinkle cornmeal or baking soda on the sticky residue and rub, and rub with a dry cloth. Add more cornmeal or baking soda as needed. This will not mar the finish.

Before reusing a planter, wash the pot thoroughly in side and out with hot soapy water. Then soak the planter for 5 minutes in a solution of three-quarters cup of liquid chlorine bleach to a gallon warm water; rinse well. The clorine solution disinfects the container and prevents transfer of mold or disease from the previous plant.

To take gum out of clothes, freeze and chip off.

Peanut butter will take gum out of hair.

Use hair spray to take out ball point pen ink.

To remove wax from table cloths, put paper towels on underside of material and brown paper on top. Iron with hot iron.

Bleach kills mildew, but to prevent it from returning use silcone gel or calcium chloride granules to retard growth.

Carpet Spot Removal

When using ammonia for spot removal always dilute with ten parts of water.

Detergents (Trend, Vel, Dreft, Ivory) dilute 20 to 1 with water.

Dry cleaning fluid (Carbona, Renuzit, Energine or Perk) use straight from container.

Distilled white vinegar dilute 50 to 50 with water.

For Alcoholic Beverages: Apply detergent solution, blot. Apply vinegar solution, blot. Apply ammonia solution, blot. Bleach with 3% to 5% hydrogen peroxide or sodium perborate. Rinse with water and blot dry.

For Butter and Margarine: Apply dry cleaning solvent, blot. Apply detergent solution, blot. Rinse and blot dry.

For Blood: Scrape off surface. Apply cool detergent solution, blot. Apply cool ammonia solution, blot. Rinse and blot dry. Apply rust remover, followed by 3% to 5% hydrogen peroxide if stain remains.

For Candle Wax: Scrape off surface. Apply dry cleaning solvent, blot and repeat.

For Catsup and Tomato Sauce: Apply cool detergent or ammonia solution, bloth. If stains remains, apply 3% to 5% hydrogen peroxide, rinse, blot dry.

For Chewing Gum: If hard or solid, apply commercial gum freeze. (Ice cube in a plastic bag will work sometimes.) Hold on gum until it becomes brittle. Break into pieces and vacuum. Apply dry cleaning solvent to residue.

For Chocolate: Rub with a paste of raw egg yolk, rinse. If stain if old, apply a few drops of denature alcohol, rinse.

For Jam and Jelly: Apple detergent solution, blot. Apply vinegar solution, blot. Rinse and blot dry.

For Mildew: Apply solution of 1 tsp. disinfectant cleaner to 1 C. water, blot. Apply ammonia solution, blot. Rinse and blot dry. Keep area dry.

For Milk, Cream or Ice Cream: Apple ammonia solution and rinse. If area is large, shampoo afterwards.

For Mustard: Apply detergent solution, blot. Apply vinegar solution, blot. If stain remains apply rust remover or hydrogen peroxide solution, blot. Do not use ammonia or alkalies.

For Iodine Mercurochrome or Merthiolate: Apply denatured alcohol, blot. Rinse and blot. Some stain may remain.

For Grease or Oil: Apply paint thinner or Perk. Work to center to avoid ring, blot. Apply light detergent solution and rinse.

Camp
Cookin'

.......because camp cooks need to be immersed in lake water more than in dish water.

Mary Ann Kerl

$9.95 + $3.00 S/H

VENISON COOKBOOK

FOUR WHEELIN'

SLUG SLINGIN'

BEER DRINKIN'

ARROW SHOOTIN'

HELL RAISIN'

A REAL HE-MAN COOKBOOK WITH RECIPES
THAT USE DEAD THINGS, AND HOT STUFF,
AND PARTS OF PICKUP TRUCKS.

BY RICK BLACK

$9.95 + $3.00 S/H

The
FUNKY DUCK
Duck COOKBOOK

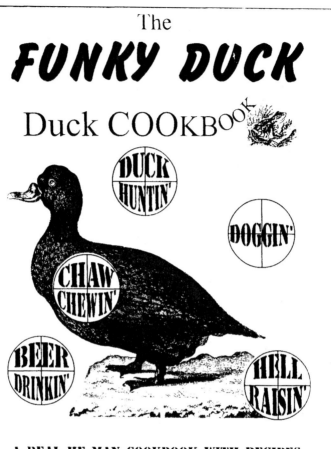

DUCK HUNTIN'

DOGGIN'

CHAW CHEWIN'

BEER DRINKIN'

HELL RAISIN'

**A REAL HE-MAN COOKBOOK WITH RECIPES
THAT USE DEAD THINGS, AND HOT STUFF,
AND PARTS OF PICKUP TRUCKS.**

**WITH THIS COOKBOOK, YOU CAN BE
A REAL HE-MAN!**

BY RICK BLACK

$9.95 + $3.00 S/H

(187)

BAG 'EM

and

TAG 'EM

-all about deer huntin'

by Rick Black

$9.95 + $3.00 S/H

COOKIN'

WITH

BEER

Anybody can sit there drinkin' beer 'til the cows come home ... or go to work ... or whatever it is that cows do.

The real connsure ...conneusjour ... conus .... the real cool guy is the one who uses beer as an ingredient in cookin'.

You'll find, in this book, some recipes that'll absolutely knock your socks off .... and some other stuff you'll want to keep out of the hands of women, children and Republicans.

By Rick Black

$9.95 + $3.00 S/H

(189)

NOW, WHADDA WE DO WITH THIS

DEAD DEER

COOKBOOK
and
How-to Book

So, you shot him! . . . Now whadda do with
him . . ?, all about field dressing, transporting
your deer, special concerns about preparing it
for the taxidermist, etc. etc. . . . and some
great recipes.

Rick Black

$9.95 + $3.00 S/H

the
TURKEY
COOKBOOK

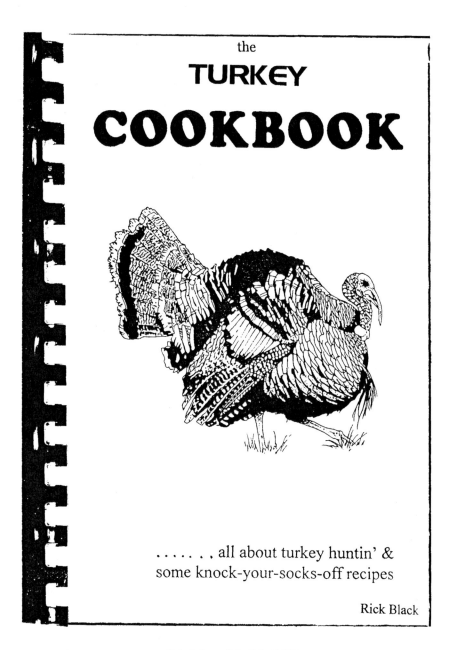

. . . . . . , all about turkey huntin' &
some knock-your-socks-off recipes

Rick Black

$9.95 + $3.00 S/H

The

VEGETARIAN
WILD GAME
COOKBOOK

Recipes for really great dishes using
only those game animals that are

PURELY   VEGETARIAN

See, you can be politically correct without giving up those
great steaks or barbequed stuff . . . . and we know how important it is for you to be politically correct.

Rick Black

$9.95 + $3.00 S/H

(192)

the

WESTERN
FRONTIER
COOK
BOOK

. . . . recipes that come down to
us from the Great American Frontier

by Stoney Hardcastle

$9.95 + $3.00 S/H

MOUNTAIN MAN

COOK BOOK

..... vittle's that'll make you as tough as a gnawin' and clawin', spittin' and snarlin' two hundred pound mountain lion ..... almost as tough as one of America's most colorful characters . . . The Mountain Man

By: Rick Black

$9.95 + $3.00 S/H

INDIAN
COOKING
COOK BOOK

— *according to the practices of the:*
LAKOTA
CHIPPEWA
CHEROKEE
OTTOWA
CREE

by Bruce Carlson

$9.95 + $3.00 S/H

The
Cow Puncher's
COOKBOOK

A collection of "Outdoor Cooking" recipes with an Old Western Flair. Like ole Cookie sez, "Iffen ya ain't et outa cast iron, ya ain't et yet."

by Fred Carlson

$9.95 + $3.00 S/H

The

HUNTING

in the

NUDE

COOKBOOK

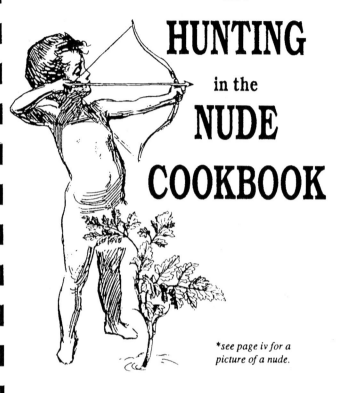

*see page iv for a
picture of a nude.*

- Flat out Double-Good Wild Game Cookin'
- And some things to think about as you
  consider stompin' around in fields and
  forests ... in the nude.

by Bruce Carlson

$9.95 + $3.00 S/H

SOUTHWESTERN NATIVE AMERICAN COOKING

by Barb Soden

$9.95 + $3.00 S/H

Alicia Stoller: Cover Illustrator
Maddi Nafziger: Text Illustrator

by Rick Black

$9.95 + $3.00 S/H

the
RV
COOKBOOK

Great Recipes for Folks
on the Go

by
Bob Fugate

$9.95 + $3.00 S/H

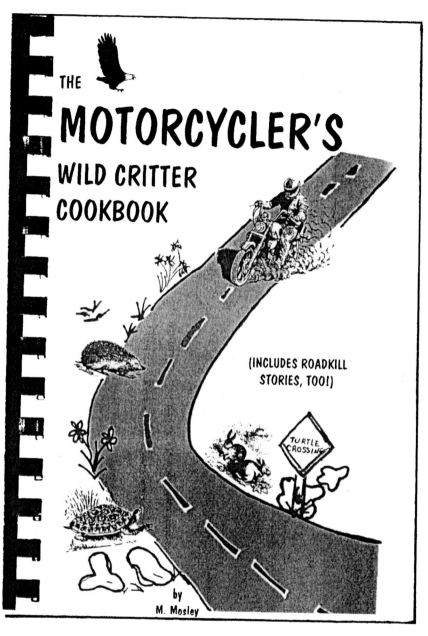

THE

MOTORCYCLER'S
WILD CRITTER
COOKBOOK

(INCLUDES ROADKILL
STORIES, TOO!)

TURTLE
CROSSING

by
M. Mosley

$9.95 + $3.00 S/H

FEASTS
MOONS

(Wii-Kon-Ge-Inizan Maazina 'igans)

This book shows the various North American Indians' names for
the different months of the year . . . . . . along with recipes appro-
priate for each of these months. Recipes are given both in original form, and in modern form.

$9.95 + $3.00 S/H

OUTDOOR COOKING

for

Outdoor Men

Game or Tame

"OK, Buster, you shot it outside, so now you can cook it outside."

by Rick Black

$9.95 + $3.00 S/H

COOKIN'
Pan Fish

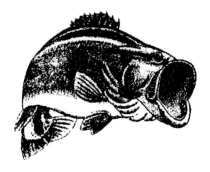

Lotsa Great Recipes
about

..... "settin' fire" to God's second greatest gift
to mankind.

..... plus some super fishin' hints as well as a
couple dumb jokes.

Rick Black

Bird Up!

Pheasant Cookbook 'n more

How to shoot 'em & how to cook 'em . . . . . along
with dog care hints, safety, sharing our vision with
the kids & other good stuff and . . . . .

we haven't forgotten **Quail & Grouse**. There's
some good quail & grouse stuff here too.

By Rick Black

(205)

CatfisH

(from C to H)

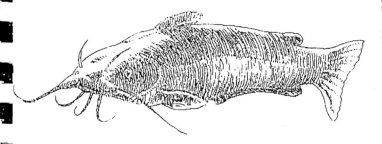

How to Hook 'em
&
How to Cook 'em

This book tells you everything you ever wanted to know about how to catch and how to cook those creatures from the brown lagoon . . . . and probably some stuff you could care less about.

by Rick Black

RECIPES

Cooking practices of the Ute
from many years ago.

by Shari Ray

$9.95 + $3.00 S/H

OJIBWAY

RECIPES

Cooking practices of the Ojibway
from many years ago.

by Kim Becwar
Lyle Ernst

$9.95 + $3.00 S/H

(208)

HO-CHUNK
RECIPES

Cooking practices of the Ho-Chunk
from many years ago.

by Kim Becwar
Lyle Ernst

$9.95 + $3.00 S/H

To Order Copies

Please send me _____ copies of *Wild Critter* at $11.95 each plus $3.50 S/H. (Make checks payable to Quixote Press.)

Name _____

Street _____

City _____ State _____ Zip _____

Black Iron Cooking
(a dinky division of Quixote Press)
3544 Blakslee Street
Wever IA 52658
1-800-571-2665

To Order Copies

Please send me _____ copies of *Wild Critter* at $11.95 each plus $3.50 S/H. (Make checks payable to Quixote Press.)

Name _____

Street _____

City _____ State _____ Zip _____

Black Iron Cooking
(a dinky division of Quixote Press)
3544 Blakslee Street
Wever IA 52658
1-800-571-2665